# PEACE
## AND
# LOVE

**an oblique view of the demons within**

*Fulford Chin Choy*

ISBN: 1-4196-7764-0
ISBN-13: 978-1419677649
Library of Congress Control Number: 2007906965

Visit www.booksurge.com to order additional copies.

*In the process of scribbling the words within I learned to appreciate more the love of my wife Monica, and our children, Roxanne and Marc. Expressing my thoughts into appropriate words was a challenge from the start. With the guiding assistance, countless times, of Roxanne as well as Margaret Williams, I believe that was achieved. My grateful thanks also to my many friends and acquaintances for their comments ,and insights, on the varied qualities of human nature.*

# Contents

# *Preface*

Writing, they say, is an art. But rarely are writers called artists. Rather they prefer to be known as authors. As for me, I write for the fun of it. I guess this, to some, might identify me as a jester. That's the shortcoming with generalizing and then labelling others. Preferably, we ought to accept others as they are, namely, as individuals with each a mind-set of her/his own as well as unique traits including, at times, perhaps strange, personal reasons for certain actions. Similarly, the emotional makeup of an individual varies from one person to the next. Understanding such emotional pulls and sways begins with an introspective reflection of one's own ways and habits. Over many years I did precisely that. What certainly helped was my service, as a draftee, in the U.S. Army as well as, much later, being a member of an employment equity task force for an Ontario Ministry. Thereafter I decided to record, onto paper, over many years, such reflections. Hopefully, what I have written may be of help to someone who wish to do a step-by-step analysis towards understanding the emotional side to human nature. The first step, in the process, begins with an introspection of one's personal experience particularly while growing up. Needless to say, by doing so there commonly is unleashed emotional demons as one recalls the past. Each puzzling thought usually leads to more complex issues, such as why should I change ? Why don't others, instead, adjust to my behaviour? But such accommodating actions are what

1

everyone else apparently wants. Why do these demons exist ? The cause is within our very being. These demons have been described so aptly as the seven deadly sins. Counteracting them is not easy; but it can be done. What is written should assist the reader on a personal journey and quest towards such understanding and self control. My suggestion is to read just a paragraph or two then reflect and consider one's own situation. As a matter of fact the reader can, if so inclined, skip and wander through the pages since each paragraph is self contained. Take a look at the CONTENTS then go to a topic of interest. Trust that, while doing so, you will encounter food for thoughtful reflections and, hopefully, constructive personal action. Bon appétit.

# Why Seek The Demons Within

With the new millennium there seems to be a change to the social order. Out goes the colonial way of life. Out go the overriding values of western culture and their influence. Such styles of the twentieth century are now history. Just take a peek at the various chat rooms and web sites on the internet. Global diversity is now a part of the social fabric. With diversity, however, comes a bit of uncertainty. Some may even say chaos. Quite a few thus prefer adhering to the old ways of doing things. But to believe that this will return to the fore is wishful thinking rather than reality. To face what is now in vogue may need, more than ever, a greater degree of self-confidence, confidence based on a greater awareness of one's emotional strengths and limitations. Such confidence would help an individual to cope with the stress that living today brings.

In today's world stress is common. In addition, camaraderie seems to be missing, many times, whenever people interact. Both seem to be factors that cause a greater degree of hardship as well as adversity. Often this brings about a chilling feeling, much like being overpowered by a sinister dark force. Sometimes the intensity is such that there is a sense of despair, even paranoid behaviour. Such an outlook can be discerned in people at schools, workplaces and homes, even at play. To cope many feel that they need the ability, agility, and energy of a superman. On that note it is interesting to mention that superman of the comics genre has now 'died'. What hope do mere mortals have in meeting the challenge of such trying circumstances ?

Still, life goes on. Each day many live in hope of a better tomorrow. Hope, they say, springs eternal from the human breast. But try telling that to those who have lost all hope. As for a better tomorrow, some seem to believe that winning a lottery will solve all their problems. Well, the results to date show that winning a lottery can create more problems. Then what should a person do ? There are no easy answers. Nonetheless one ought to explore ways and means so as to reduce one's personal level of stress. To do that likely necessitates that one try and overcome any inertia or personal malaise and try not continuing bad habits and behaviour. Such tendencies, once in action, usually cause, afterwards, a sense of guilt. To overcome these tendencies, however, would take more than wishful thinking. For often they are so ingrained that they are part of one's natural reaction to a certain set of circumstances. So it will likely take more than a mental notion to do things differently the next time around. Wanting to change and attempting to do something about it is the first step towards overcoming bad habits and behaviour. Taking that first step, however, is what many avoid.

Many times people will start out with a firm resolution to change their bad habits, to stop what they consider to be contrary to anyone's expectations. Their resolve to stop might actually happen on the first go. But, eventually, many likely falter. Is kicking a habit hard ? It certainly is, as many can testify. But usually nothing worthwhile gaining is easy. As for falling back into old habits, quite a few would attribute this to an excuse normally questionable to others. A common one is to blame others. Others were the cause due to, for instance, a lack of moral support. In essence, they were evading the yoke of taking responsibility for their actions. Seemingly overlooked is that the process of change has to start with one coming face to face with the prime mover. That's easy to do. All one needs to do is to stand in front of a mirror. To thyself be true. The next step is to do a critical mental review of how the behaviour got started in the first place, to consider the underlying causes. Then do something about it. Keep in mind that whenever there is a **WILL** then there is a way. Remember, NO PAIN, NO GAIN. The good news is that the pain is not physical. The bad news is that the pain, if any, is mental. What it now takes is determination. Courage too. Courage to face the sordid truth.

The feeling of stress varies in degree from one person to the next, whether the stress be mental or physical. What is stressful to some may not be stressful to others. But all know the feeling that comes during a stressful situation - the heartbeat rising, the breathing getting heavy. There may even be a sense of dread. Stress makes you tense. Sometimes the tension makes you nervous. Sometimes stress makes your sense of hearing very keen. So keen you can hear the drop of a pin. You are also able to see every tiny movement within your line of vision. Many, under stress, hope that the world would somehow continue in the old familiar way, as it always did umpteen times before, but to no avail. Stress also triggers an alarm response of the bodily functions. The adrenal glands start pumping more hormones. Often you feel the adrenaline rush. The body is now ready to cope with the level of stress experienced. But there is a price to pay. There is now a shrinkage of the thymus, spleen and lymph nodes. This shrinkage causes these nodes to decrease production of immunization cells. It seems like the hormones and the nodes are sharing a limited and fixed amount of energy. Stress makes the hormones use up much of the reserve. Naturally, in turn, there is less energy for the nodes to make immunization cells as need be, like taking from Peter to pay Paul. In addition, stress causes a decrease of eosinophils, one of the group of disease fighting white blood cells. So how does the body cope with stress ? It's simple. The body needs rest to recover, rest to replenish the energy reserve, to once more supply immunization cells as need be. The trouble is that a person with worry on her/his mind often cannot rest properly. Thus the energy reserve may stay low and have less to serve the body. The impact is that stress, over an extended period, can cause chronic illnesses such as insomnia and fatigue. It could even lead to high blood pressure or bleeding ulcers of the stomach. In other words, stress can impair one's health. Permanently.

Stress commonly clouds the thinking process. Logic seems secondary in decisions made. It is as if the mind is obsessed about the worrisome problem at hand, until it is resolved, one way or another, for better or for worse. Once that comes to pass a person usually discerns quite a few simple and appropriate solutions. *Why didn't I think of that? Why did I make such a stupid move? What was I thinking about?* And so on. It is definitely more beneficial to alleviate stress as much as you can. For example, don't put off for tomorrow what can be done today, especially should there be time available to do so. Procrastination has been the downfall of many. Moreover, stress makes people do less than their best. More importantly, stress robs a person of an opportunity to gain the power of positive thinking.

Ordinarily a person tries to tolerate, without medication, the early signs of being sick. Only when the symptoms become severe would a medical practitioner be consulted. Having stress is handled in much the same way, namely, only when the symptoms become chronic would a doctor, even a specialist, be consulted. So the good doctor arranges a series of medical tests, which the patient is often more than willing to do, giving blood and urine samples, letting medics subject their body to all sorts of probes, receptors and prodding, as well as taking any related discomfort patiently. Often there is a sense of relief, perhaps stemming from a sense of hope that a cure is on the way. The next step in the drama is when the good doctor explains the results from all these tests. Usually medication is prescribed. A few might need to take the medication for the rest of their life. In most cases they are told to change their personal lifestyle: sleep properly; watch what they eat; and exercise regularly. For the next few months they may try all three. But after that, for some, old habits are hard to break. Once they start feeling better then there is nothing wrong, they believe, with reverting back to their old lifestyle. What the patient forgot to make, however, is a very important change, namely, a change to their mental frame of mind about their outlook on life. By adopting a new life-style there may be a long-term cure for the stress experienced.

Whether one likes it or not, stress is a part of life. As a matter of fact a life free of stress can be boring. In that regard they say that stress, now and then, is good for the body. I guess this keeps the adrenaline system primed and in good working condition, ready for a real emergency. As a matter of fact many accept that stress always will be an integral part of their life. So they try to take appropriate measures to cope with stress, such as following a regimen of routine physical workout. But doing physical exercise alone is no guarantee that they will not have any chronic illness caused by stress, such as having difficulty falling asleep though they may be very tired. Coping with stress also requires a settled personal disposition, a tranquil mind. But such a frame of mind, for some, seems somewhere over the rainbow. To reach this state of mind one needs tolerance and understanding: a tolerance for others; a deep understanding of one's inner self and positive traits, such as how to communicate, effectively, one's thinking; and a realization about how the primal emotional instincts sway the way people do what they do.

With such understanding one has a chance to be positive in one's thinking, to have greater self-control, a cerebral control which builds on one's insights, for instance, into why others do what they do. Eventually, then, one can accept, without questioning openly, the actions of others. More importantly, one should not forget nature's medicine to relieve stress, which is nothing less than laughter. Laughter, for example, relaxes the facial muscles. To take that medicine, however, one needs a sense of humour.

# *Growing Up - The Emotional Phase*

The emotional phase of our existence lasts a lifetime. During the adolescent stage it can be very challenging and, at times, tumultuous. An occasional incident might leave an indelible mark. Many aspects to this experience are noted on the following pages. To some readers, however, what is noted occasionally will be boring. But what is boring to one reader may be appropriate to another. Trust that you will be selective by scanning the topical captions beforehand. One thought to keep in mind is that the emotional phase is a never-ending learning process as to the breadth and depth of human nature.

## *an item ordinarily not in one's day to day agenda*

In this planet of ours there are a varied multitude of living species. There is the almost invisible world of microbes. These are very tiny creatures which multiply at a relatively rapid rate. For instance, a bacterium common in our daily food chain has a generation span of about fifteen minutes. There are also the fishes and many other life forms swimming in the sea, as well as the fauna and flora of the botany domain. Similarly around are the animals and creatures of the land. Then there are humans. Though there are physiological differences between all the species they share one thing in common, namely, growth. Starting with life the size of less than a dot they grow to a youthful vigour. Thereafter comes puberty and, life permitting, old age. As to the stage each life form will reach, that seems to be determined by individual lot and the luck of the draw. In this respect death can strike at any time and spares no stage of the life cycle. Death is the eventual fate of each and everyone around. Regardless of this fact, however, people ordinarily live and plan their personal life and future as if the inevitable end is not near, even on the morrow, as if they themselves won't be one of those who dies suddenly and unexpectantly. They live as if, for sure, they won't be one of those who expires before doing all they would like before their demise, such as saying goodbye to everyone they want to beforehand, as if they are going to live life to the full. Such wishful thinking is common, probably as much as some believing that they have very little control over their own fate. They believe their individual journey through this life is charted mostly by circumstances as well as by the decisions made by others. But no matter how circumstances, or others, play a part, they have control over the decisions they make, especially the way they react to events unfolding around them as well as to what others do while interacting with them. It is really up to each person to decide what action to take, whether, for instance, one reacts with malice or with love, perhaps not to take any action at all. One would then just let the chips fall as they may, including what happens after one dies. That is likely what takes place with many whether by design or by ignorance. Possibly they ought to give a thought to how they would like others to remember them, whether, for instance, in a positive and favourable light or as an irksome character.

## SEEING THING DIFFERENTLY

*life can be tough*
*putting away childish ways*
*the parental issue*

It is natural for one to daydream. The world of daydreams probably emerges once an individual acquires an imaginative mind. Funny that children, in their daydreams, often fantasize about themselves as adults, such as an actor, or a great sports figure, even a *'wonder woman'* or a superman. Sometimes this fantasy takes hold whenever an elder, such as a parent, reprimands children for what they did or maybe for what they are about to do. If they were grown up no one would dare talk to them that way. Ah, the freedom grown ups have. They can do as they please. Well, in no time, or so it seems, the teenage years end and the adult world comes to pass. How quickly, in retrospect, time flies. Thus ended the days of youthful reverie. The carefree years are no longer to be. However, there is a rude awakening. There are now big-time responsibilities. No more can they take food and shelter for granted. Such survival needs are for them to secure. Now they need to fend for themselves. Now they have to seek out a source of income, to look for and secure a job. Once that's done and settled, however, there crops up the need to maintain an abode as well as to cultivate a social life. On each of these subjects there seems to be hardly enough time, energy and money to do what they have in mind: places to go, people to see, things to do. Often they lose touch with some close friends. Many gain too much weight from a lack of proper and adequate exercise. There seems to be a flustered feeling, at times, from not being able to do all that is on their wish list. Occasionally, for instance, there would be two fabulous functions to attend but taking place on the same day if not at the same time. Indeed, it is common to feel fraught with anxiety. As children, in their wildest dreams, such a social dilemma hardly was anticipated. *'If only it was possible to return to the carefree world of a child'* is the daydream many adults have.

In many societies of old there was a ceremony for an individual to confirm the rite of passage. This ceremony bestows on an adolescent the status of adulthood. In the society of today the rite of passage has no such formal ceremony except for a few ethnic groups. The actual rite of passage, in today's society, seems to be referred to merely as growing up. It is likely just an observed personality change from mostly childish behaviour to a more mature demeanour. As to when this takes place, well that very likely varies from one adolescent to the next. As a matter of fact quite a few, even in old age, in the opinion of some, have yet to grow up. Growing up is far from being a biological transitional moment, or even a specific point in one's journey through life, such as when a person graduates from high school. Growing up can be an awkward experience and probably happens only when an individual is good and ready to do so. Perhaps when they have a desire, and are willing, to put some sort of order in their personal lives. Usually when this comes to mind many tend to seek the advice and wisdom of those they trust. Growing up is a frame of mind that views life quite differently from that of a child: doing what, knowingly, is constructive; considering the many choices available before they take action; personally taking control over what they can and are able to do; and being willing to accept, at times reluctantly, the consequences of their personal actions, even if that should be to do nothing. Most of all, growing up is a very personal rite of passage which involves one willingly taking responsibility for whatever one does. Make no mistake, many personal oversights and errors are going to be made. That is innate to human nature. As the saying goes, to err is human.

From the moment of birth a child yearns for nurturing and care. For those fortunate enough, a parent is there to provide this with loving attention. With further good fortune a loving relationship between them may extend into the adolescent years and even beyond, sometimes even after the adolescent has matured and is on her/his own. What a child ordinarily lacks, entering maturity, is experience. Well, many a parent is more than willing to fill that gap. They are willing to give advice, often without being asked, and to provide supportive supervision so as to ensure the child carries out the suggested course of action. The common reaction of the child, naturally, is to protest about such attentiveness. They more than often declare that they are capable of making their own decision. Such parental 'help', to the child, is somewhat like a taut umbilical cord. Worse yet should a child protest too much. A common retort of the parent to such a display of displeasure is to pontificate that their involvement is **for your own good**. But what the parent fails to see is that giving advice is one thing and letting the child decide what to do is another. The child, after all, has a will of her/his own. In situations where the parent continues to prevail the child might reluctantly consider the parent as someone who must be obeyed. In addition, what the parent fails to understand, or doesn't want to, is that she/his is exercising excessive control. Furthermore, although the parent has the best of intentions, the child has to learn how to cope on her/his own. In due course nearly everyone, sooner or later, finds a way to break this parental bond of control. Often for that to happen one has to perceive one's parents as somebody with faults and foibles, to accept this as well as the fact that parent had the best of intentions. Even at this stage, however, there could be moments of disagreement. Often it is the offspring who gets angry and upset. There is an explanation: many parents know how to control such a situation. Parents, more than anyone else, know which buttons to push to get their offspring angry and adrenaline charged. Parents know how to make their offspring, although grown up, lose their cool. Quite a few parents, consciously or not, would deliberately do so. Parents are quick, in such resulting situations, to then point out how no respect is being shown to them. This then causes the offspring to feel guilty. The challenge at such times, for the offspring, is not to lose control and let their emotions take over. One ought to show parents a personal level of tolerance greater than humanly possible, to remind parents that their advice would be given consideration, and that such advice comes with the best of intentions, which only a loving parent can give. However one has an opinion of one's own including how things ought to be done, even if that has certain risks. For sometimes, in life, that is necessary. For sometimes a decision that needs to be taken might differ from the conservative opinion of a parent.

## UNDER A SPELL

*a gap in personal values*
*a youthful mind-set*
*personal point of view*
*generalization*
*to know it all*

From the moment of birth a baby starts to learn how to cope. Babies know that, under ordinary circumstances, by kicking and screaming someone would feed them and look after them. Shortly thereafter they gain insight and knowledge through their bodily senses. For instance, it may be noticed by anyone observant how keenly babies take in everything with their eyes. Likewise, how quickly babies coordinate the many sounds they hear with the related visual images. Similarly coordinated are the data gained through smelling, touching and tasting. All this is absorbed like a sponge. All this is collated in the memory banks of the brain. Of course, the process continues from infancy into adolescence and beyond. Growth in childhood, physical as well as mental, seems to be in spurts. Along with growth comes a sense of independence and how to cope. After a while they look forward to making decisions on their own. They start out on this process on minor matters. For instance, they want to select what to wear. Similarly, they would like to decide who would be their intimate friends. During the teenage years adolescents learn that the thinking and viewpoint of their home differs somewhat from that of their peer group. Usually the home parental values are ethical, constructive, long-term and lasting in nature. But usually those of their peer group are self-gratifying, playful and tinted with gamesmanship. This conflicting situation is often the cause of the **generation gap**. Still, many adolescents try and respect the family values of home while catering to the casual values of their peers. But many times curiosity and a hunger for excitement gets the better of adolescents. They might then naively pursue their curiosity. This could cause them to listen to people with radical views and unconventional values. It might also lead youths to follow a path of life and thinking outside the norm. Most, after just a taste of such pathways, would return to mainstream society. However, a few would continue their deviant experience. Which path an adolescent pursues, usually innocently at the start, seems to be more impulsive than a thoughtful choice. Fate and luck may come into play.

There are moments in life when one's mind is clear, lucid and receptive, when one is eager to learn. Such moments are many during one's teenage years. Probably this is nature's way to prepare adolescents for the transition from dependence on parents and guardians alike to the adult world of being on their own. A common display of such independence comes to the fore whenever a youth tries to do things in her/his own enigmatic way. But being endowed with such learning perceptiveness is one side to the equation. On the other side is how a youth puts this ability to use. Usually youths do so from a point of personal interest. Fortunately, many do so pursuing academic studies and sporting endeavours. But often adolescents have a curious interest in a social phenomenon outside of their immediate norm. For instance, a youth might be attracted to a charismatic character, such as an entertaining pop star, perhaps an inspiring mentor, maybe a religious zealot. Or, worse yet, a two bit guru who captivates the youth's imagination and zest. Sometimes a youth decides to explore such a social phenomenon. In the process they may become deeply involved. What they experience then could likely influence their outlook on life. Hopefully, adolescents stay within the mainstream after this growing up phase. As Wordsworth so aptly puts it, 'The Child is father of the Man'.

A common personal response to an interpersonal situation, in public, is to go with the flow. Many do so whenever they try and conform with social customs and prevailing conventions. But while doing so they may have personal opinions and preferences of their own, much like the food an individual might prefer, whether that be hot and spicy or bland and mild, or perhaps betwixt. It commonly depends on what was experienced at home. Likewise the opinions an individual holds usually originated from what they hear at home. Home is commonly where one learns one's moral and social values, values which usually reflect the ethnic culture of the parents, tempered, of course, with what they later learn during their formative teens.

Sometimes this might be tinted with religious fervour. Thus an individual very likely has a unique point of view which is a hybrid of many sources, a point of view which the individual then uses to judge the actions of others. The challenge is to understand that others may have a different but likely valid point of view. Therefore the challenge one faces, but might overlook, is to tolerate what others do. More so should they respect the laws of the land and the individual rights of others. Otherwise one is imposing a personal point of view, without justification, upon someone who thinks differently.

Interpersonal relations are a phenomenon which people continue to learn more about as long as they live. This phenomenon affects a person at every phase of life. A tot, for instance, would, upon encountering someone new and strange, very likely run to the comfort of the mother's embrace. A tot also learns quickly who to trust and who to fear amid the intimate circle of family and friends. As for the adolescent phase, that's when people would get accustomed to meeting and getting acquainted with others on their own. In the process, naturally, they form an opinion of each character they get to know. Sometimes it is favourable. Sometimes it is not. Many times these characters are, in time, so familiar that their traits are taken for granted. But for the general public it is a different story. Generalization is the common order of the day. People usually are lumped into parcels of groups such as by social strata or by religious congregation or by ethnic background. This is the by-product of stereotype by generalization. Many times, however, such labels, which are imagined to be true, are construed mostly from erroneous hearsay. Luckily people usually would forego such stereotyping once they develop mutual friendship with someone from such a grouping. The challenge an adolescent faces is to realize that people are individuals, that no two persons are alike, no matter of what ethnic background or religious fervour. Each person has a character, whether good or bad, all her/his own. Alas, there are many who, even in old age, continue to group certain people with specific labels and unjustified traits.

During the teenage years one becomes exposed to constantly new ideas and experiences. All this is assimilated and collated sometimes with little effort, sometimes after thoughtful reflection. In the process insights and knowledge are gained. Some see, with awe, beauty and efficiency in the logic of the matters learned. Some marvel at the thoroughness of the many processes studied. Others are puzzled by the inconsistency and limitations. Moreover a few would, in their opinion, figure out better ways and means. All these mental gymnastics are part of the learning process during the teenage years. Sometimes, however, this makes an adolescent a constant critic of others. They might, for instance, point out the clumsiness and oversights of elders, questioning what appears to be outdated habits and customs. All this questioning might, just might, make an individual belittle those who adhere to such habits and customs. This could even fuel, in these few, an inner sense of personal superiority. They seem to feel that they know more. Often this leads to a frame of mind, likely a superiority complex, usually shown by seemingly having an answer for everything. They behave as someone whose middle name is KNOW-IT-ALL, as if they are capable of doing everything better than anyone else. Such a frame of mind tends to make an individual act arrogantly. Likewise they seem to be intolerant of others, particularly towards those who criticize them and who may have opposing views. Such an individual is somewhat narrow-minded and provincial in their thinking. Sadly there are a few who think like this even in old age. To go beyond this stunted phase one has to acknowledge that other viewpoints also could be valid, if not more meaningful. After all, there is more than one way to skin a cat. Furthermore, one never stops learning during one's lifetime.

## LIFE CAN BE AN EMOTIONAL ROLLER COASTER

*having a sense of humour*
*the emotional lows*
*wanting this and wanting that*

There are times in life when nothing new appeals to one's interest. In fact the moment could be filled with a feeling of blah, somewhat like one being under a sinister cloud and bored. What one very likely desires, at that moment, is to recharge one's battery with personal energy. What a contrast this is to those moments when one is filled with elation and feels on top of the world, days when everything goes one's way, days when even the weather prevails with sun-filled joy, pleasant moments with a thrill much like that which comes with being a dad for the first time. Then again there are days also when one is down, despondent and blue, when one feels like crawling into a dark crevice and hiding there, much like the gloom which comes with a personal disaster. Let's face it, such varied moments show that life carries a mix bag of ups and downs. Life has many emotional highs and lows. Altogether these are experienced on the emotional roller-coaster of life. A roller coaster that, at times, encounters crossed signals, such as when a person sheds a tear of joy, or when an individual, although immersed in grief, laughs upon observing a funny human situation. The roller coaster ride also has periods of humdrum routine. Periods during which a person savours a monotonous daily diet of work, eat and sleep, a diet which stretches often from one week to the next. Any break to the monotony is busily occupied with personal chores and social obligations. Rarely is there time to smell the roses. If only one could find a way to relax. If only one could garner a pause which refreshes. To do that one might have to tap into an innate human trait within. One may need to bring consciously to the fore a natural morale-booster. This is a personal sense of humour. With this one can perceive the funny side to human behaviour in the actions of people around. With this one can discern an irony occurring within a serious situation. Through humour one gets an opportunity to loosen, even for just a moment, any inner tension caused by stress. Through humour one might see the lighter side to being alive and not take life too seriously. But all this cannot come about unless one endeavours to do so with a conscious effort.

For many hard-working individuals there are periodic spells during which they feel overwhelmed by chronic personal issues, such as a nagging dispute with someone else, or a terrible situation which refuses to go away, issues which make some wonder why, of all people, this was happening to them. At such times it is natural to dread that what could go wrong will go wrong. As to the many chronic issues, a common one stems from spending a bit more than one can afford. To make ends meet, a person usually utilizes the limits on various credit cards, charging each to the hilt. But paying by plastic, without any thought as to the debt, is going to put a person deeper in the hole. Trying to make ends meet is going to take more than a prayer and a hope. One likely will need to make personal sacrifice. One must give up costly and expensive spending habits. As a matter of fact, to pay off the debt, one has to spend less than one can afford. To do so one has to change one's mind-set as well as one's ways and habits. More than likely such a course of action might be needed to resolve any other chronic personal issue. In all cases, to resolve the situation would depend on an individual's willingness to change. It depends on a willingness to make do with what she/he has. It depends on a willingness, more importantly, to face the responsibility for one's actions, as well as any consequences. That process of change starts from within. That process starts with, for example, tolerating the irritating faults in others. One could kick-start the change process by planning ahead personal actions. By thinking through the activities, beforehand, one might be able to chart each action in an orderly and logical fashion. By doing so one has started the change process, hopefully, to a more constructive way of life.

Historically not so long ago the variety in merchandise was somewhat limited. Either shoddy and cheap or common and dull or expensive and showy. Hours of work, for most, were nine to five. Entertainment was mostly radio, movies and television, only in black and white. Life then, in retrospect, was relatively quite simple and predictable. Well, things have changed. Now people are working every hour, every day and even every night, part time, full time, or short term contract. Now merchandise comes in every style and fashion. Now it's tough to tell the cheap goods from the high-priced ones. Entertainment too comes in every hue and whatever imaginable. Variety seems to be the spice of life. All these permutations and combinations of the market are mind-blowing. Just look at the outfits and wardrobes people wear on the streets and on public transport, especially the subways. Often this makes many feel that they have been living a sheltered life. Furthermore, nothing anymore seems to be used until worn out. For there are so many new toys, especially for adults, constantly coming on the market - more reason for one to look beyond these fads and fashions. Besides, many of these items don't stay around for too long - more reason for one to go beyond a materialistic way of life. It is more worthwhile to try and be at peace with oneself, a peace that might bring about an inner calm, a calm that usually brings with it a good night's rest. The search for such calm begins with looking inward and reflecting on how to live in peace with one another.

## SHORTCOMINGS AND LIMITATIONS

*it's not for one to reason why*
*when enough is enough*
*getting one's wish*

Starting with the adolescent years a common pastime is to daydream. It might be about a life better than the mundane, or about fame and fortune. Such fantasy comes easily with a fertile mind rich in imagination. Sometimes such imaginative thinking, however, creeps into the way many see and perceive others. Thus an individual might read into the actions of others intentions quite different from what the doer had in mind. Why they did what they did is not for one to say. Wanting to know why, however, is a natural curiosity. Often an outsider to the action attributes an intention that has no bearing to what the doer intended. So don't be hasty in like thinking. Such hasty thought may conjure up an intention the doer never imagined. Who knows, such an opinion may be right but, on the other hand, the opinion could be dead wrong. So rather than speculate, much less worry, about why others do what they did, we should focus our energy and thinking as to the possible consequences from the action that just took place. Keep in mind that sometimes people do things with the best of intentions, only to create unintended grief for the other party. Similarly many actions done in malice sometimes bring about a favourable outcome for the party despised. So the more we understand the characteristic of others, especially those with whom we deal, the more we are able to cope and safeguard our interest. In this respect it is suggested that you *keep your friends close but keep your foes closer*.

It's tough these days to find a job to one's liking. Once gotten it usually is a source of joy. Many slide into a satisfying job just by being at the right place at the right time. But this is like winning a lottery, a real luck of the draw. Still, many are satisfied just to land a job. As to keeping a job, well often that takes a lot of effort. For example, one never stops learning. There are many details one has to learn and remember. There are many deadlines one has to meet. Many work under such pressure even in a job to their liking. As a matter of fact, the tasks at hand can be so demanding that it often drain one's energy. Shortcomings thus may show up in the tasks done. Oversights thus might be made. Inadvertent mistakes could be many. Doubts might arise. Personal opinion may differ with working associates. All this stress might overflow into life away from work. As a result one's mind is far from being at peace. Such stressful circumstances are common at work. Worse yet, no matter how much effort one makes it might not be enough. There is a limit to what one can do. There is a limit to how much we each can do to help any organization. So, occasionally, there is a need to step back and consider the tasks at hand. Time should be spent to put the tasks in an order of priority and a rough timetable. It is a matter of ascertaining what can be done in a reasonable time. Not to do otherwise will likely create unwarranted stress and frustration.

Somewhere on a revered document there is written, for all to see and perhaps believe, that all men are created equal. If this is true, then why don't people all think alike ? Why is the grass greener in the paychecks of so many others ? This is what many consider in their trek to the daily drudgery of work. This is what many ponder, at times, as they try to better themselves through extra workload and academic studies in the evenings. They are likely motivated by a chase for an upscale lifestyle. To do so they make personal sacrifices and have little leisure moments. Then, one day, they reach the promised land. The goal is in their reach. The moment is at hand. It's joy of joys. It's fulfillment. But, with time, it becomes a constant challenge to maintain the pace. In addition, others are vying to achieve the same. Now there may be fear that the dream is about to unravel. It is akin to owning a yacht: the high cost of the yacht is one thing, but the maintenance and upkeep is just as expensive. So people ought to consider, before embarking on an ambitious career, whether the constant competitive challenge is worth their while. Some enjoy such challenges but others don't. As the saying goes, the second worst thing that can happen to you is not getting what you want. But the worst thing that could happen to you is getting what you wish for. So be careful what you wish for.

## HAVING AN OPINION

*there are givers and takers, mostly takers*
*life's too short to argue needlessly*
*common sense and science*

In one's adolescent years, and often thereafter, it is common to encounter a charismatic character, someone who sways one's viewpoint with persuasive charm and personal guile. One could become so mesmerized that one would give a great deal of thought to changing how one lives one's life. Knowingly or not, there may be a personal shift in mannerism and attire. Any harsh or derogatory comments, perchance even in jest, on this shift would not be taken kindly. But after the initial awe there could be a subsequent disenchantment for one reason or another, such as that the savant shows more self-centered penchants than expected, or shortcomings in their teachings. Naturally, there would be a crestfallen feeling. There could also be a blow to personal pride for being taken in by such flawed charisma. A similar disappointment, maybe not as dramatic, commonly happens whenever people pool their efforts with others in a joint venture. In this regard one would endeavour to deliver one's part of the bargain only to learn that the other party has no intention of fulfilling hers or his. The result is exasperation. There is often also a feeling of trust betrayed. Thereafter quite a few would take the stance of going it alone as much as they can. In today's world, however, it is difficult to avoid becoming involved with others in joint efforts. As is often the case, one can expect frequent give and take exchanges in the working relationship. For such ventures, therefore, one should not assume that new players will deliver as they ought; rather, one ought to be a bit skeptical until it is proven otherwise. For people, in general, are givers and takers, but mostly takers.

A common pastime is to watch people in action. Sometimes it is intriguing to notice how some people can make a complicated task seem so simple to do. But sometimes one is puzzled by how some people make complicated a task which seems simple to do. Why would they make it so complex ? Probably because the simple solution one perceived might never have occurred to them. That's how varied the thinking process is between each and everyone. As a matter of fact, what may seem logical and reasonable to one person might be considered by another to be far from appropriate and horrible. Having a difference in opinion is a common phenomenon. What many do about such differences, however, is quite nerve-wracking. For in spite of any vehement opposition they would continue to insist on the rectitude of their position. In the heat of any subsequent debate many have allowed their emotions to govern their actions, even though they would continue to exchange verbal points and counterpoints. As the crescendo in voices rises, however, so does the temper of the situation. This commonly could lead to blows. But how can blows resolve the discussion, much less the mind-set of the other party ? Better that both sides agree to disagree. Life's too short to argue needlessly. Besides, who knows, both opinions might well be far from the truth.

How a person generates an opinion apparently stems from her/his own one-of-a-kind personal experience, an experience which involves personal exposure to the spoken word, written page, observation, common sense, reasoning and insight. What can, of course, influence greatly the final conclusion are the emotions. Naturally, each believes that her/his opinion is based on sound and solid grounds. One such source of confidence is science. However, scientists have contradicted their own findings as more is learnt. For instance, at the turn of the twentieth century the scientific world believed that everywhere, especially the empty space of the sky above, is filled with an invisible substance called ether. Then midway through that century the scientific concept was that the empty space of the heavens was just that - a heck of a void. Lately, however, the scientific theory is that empty space in the heavens is filled with subatomic particles invisible to the eye. It was referred to as dark matter. It is considered to be dark energy, energy which apparently materializes out of nowhere. Likewise, of late, experts in other scientific fields have reached findings contrary to the concepts held. Such difference in opinions makes some hesitate about trusting the so-called experts. Rather they prefer to trust mainly information they consider to be valid plus a little bit of common sense. So how a person generates an opinion seems to involve a personal choice. At the same time the concluding opinion may differ from others. That is understandable. However, one ought to keep an open mind on the opinion one has. With an open mind one is able to learn and absorb new information relevant to the belief, although contradictory. Furthermore, there is always something new to learn each day. Besides, if one doesn't keep an open mind then one doesn't have a mind to change.

## TAKING PERSONAL STOCK

*pushing the envelope*
*been there, done that*
*staying one step ahead*

Every now and then many dwell on their fortune in life: past circumstances, present status and their hope for the future. In the process they would, to a degree, take stock of personal situation. It is strange how, in the process, quite a few would linger on minor shortcomings, shortcomings which are glaring to them but often hardly noticeable to others. Let it be said that no one is perfect. Shortcomings in people are natural and expected. Still, it can be a private pet peeve. Mine, one of many, is my poor writing skills. My initial draft is usually a string of mumbo jumbo words to which a few close friends can testify. My scribbling starts with free-flowing thoughts poorly put to prose. Rewrites are many, rethinking too. As for people in general, each and everyone has strengths, weaknesses and limitations. Each has them in different and varying degrees. For example, each has limitations in sporting abilities. Many believe that they cannot excel enough no matter how much they sweat and strain because others still do better. Nevertheless, this should not deter anyone from trying to find their limits. It is a matter of trying. For one's ultimate limitations can only be found by trying harder. Trying one's best is a never-ending sequence, a seemingly endless sequence of attempts, while one has the mental alertness and energy to do so. It is a matter of making the time to try again and again. Naturally, breaks are needed to rest. Also a person needs breaks to do personal chores and social activities. They then return to the challenge when they can, when they are willing and able to do so. And that's what practice is all about. Namely, it is a return to the challenge. Only through repeated tries and effort will it be possible to excel. Only then will it be possible to overcome any flaws in the routine. Thus it is a matter of pushing the personal envelope to the limit. By so doing one is also enhancing one's determination and will power. Naturally, there will come a time when no more progress is discernable. There will come a time, as a matter of fact, when one's ability regresses. Such is the nature of any endeavour one chooses to pursue.

Taking personal stock occurs perchance whenever one daydreams about a way of life different from the one of the moment. Often there is speculation about how past circumstances could have changed one's present fortune. Furthermore, what should one do about the present circumstances ? Maybe another career path ought to be pursued. Or one tries to further one's education. But usually such thoughts don't linger for long. For there is a pressing need to focus on one's present livelihood. So one's attention shifts once more to the usual routine. But no matter what, there are moments of boredom. At such times there is an urge to break from one's customary working habits. There is a desire for a change. Many then would dream about a vacation far away from home. But once that reverie is over then it's back to the familiar pattern at work. So one goes through the motions while the mind wanders off elsewhere. There is a loss of interest for the task at hand. Any break, even work-related training, would be welcomed. A common diversion is a course in computer software. But after such breaks the old sinking feeling returns once one gets back to work. To counteract the monotony many would ask for challenging assignments, no matter how much extra effort is necessary, just so that they can get away from the boring routine. Boredom spurs many to look for another career. However some, after resolving to seek something new, would hesitate about a career change. Apparently they are afraid of the uncertainty such a move brings. What if the change proves disastrous ? That question, unfortunately, cannot be answered until the dream is pursued. Only time and effort can tell. On the other hand quite a few who made the move would achieve greater success. A transitory phase they likely will refer to as a case of **'been there, done that.'**

Getting a job takes effort. Sometimes, with luck, very little effort is needed. But usually it takes a lot of effort and sweat. It takes time too. Time has to be spent thinking about what one is capable of doing with one's present credentials. Time has to be spent putting all this down onto paper. Time has to be spent checking the jobs available. Time has to be spent seeing how one's supply meets market demand. Rarely is there a perfect fit. Many times one's résumé suits a lowly paid position. Similarly, the jobs one desires demand more than one can offer. So innovative individuals would slant their résumé to somehow match what's wanted. Then they hope for the best. They may get lucky. With a likely sigh of relief they then enjoy the success of the quest. Often they start the job with a positive outlook. Soon, thereafter, a habitual pattern takes shape. In time, the pattern becomes a routine. Soon the protocols and processes are taken for granted. Until, for one reason or another, the job is no more. Possibly this comes about due to redundancy or downsizing, or there was a confrontation with the boss. But, no matter how legitimate the reason, that may seem trivial. *'Of all the people to lose their job, why me'.* What may follow is an inner rage. Sometimes there is a sense of gloom and doom. Perchance also there is a loss of self-esteem. Whatever sad moods are experienced, they are taken home. And there they linger for a while. For hardly anyone prepares for this moment. Much less do they know what to do about the situation. This point in time is the worst possible moment for one to sort out their personal path of fortune. That ought to be done in a calm fashion and when one's mind is clear. As a matter of fact, one ought to do the sorting when times are good. One ought then to prepare a plan for personal *'worst case'* scenario, a contingency plan they can then follow in such cases, so that, heaven forbid, should that happen then one would have a rough idea what to do next - until things hopefully get better.

## GRIEF

*time waits for no one grieving*
*the pain from grief*
*the pangs of remorse*
*bringing closure*

For nearly everyone there will come that inevitable day of grieving over the death of someone they know and regard kindly. This pain and anguish often is magnified should the person be immediate family or an intimate friend. The grief may transform one into a person filled with tension and fear, a hollow sphere where time seems to slow to a crawl. Yet everything around them would continue going on in its own merry and eerie manner. How can this be ? In a sense, one's world of yesterday has just ended. A world one very likely thought, unrealistically, never would end. But now it has. There is now an ending one never wished for. Yet every cell in their brain and every muscle in their body wants to turn back the hands on the universal clock. Instead, every pore in their body is filled with tension and an uneasy void. Now they mentally replay the many happy moments with that individual just deceased. Now they remember even the sad occasions. Oh, why can't coexistence with the past continue ? Common sense tells, alas, that this is now no longer possible. Common sense foretells that life still goes on. This is the tragic dilemma nearly everyone faces in their moment of grief. Only time can heal the wounds that opened with the death of the departed one.

Grief brings pain. For one, it is the pain of trying to halt and reverse the onward march of time, in spite of knowing that time only goes unfailingly forward, never backward. Time never retreats. In this futile attempt to turn back time individuals unlock, instead, a flood of memorable moments about the person they just lost. Moments of happier times are recalled. Comical and laughing events are remembered. Occasions of misunderstandings come to mind. Many will try to consciously erect a mental force field around the memorable times. But the realistic cells in their mind would bombard and splinter apart this imaginary shield. Soon the mind is drowned in an ocean of overwhelming grief. Soon the pain engulfs every muscle of their fatigued body. Fighting the feeling only makes the mind sink lower and deeper into a sea of despair. Despondency sets in. One way out is to let the pain engulf without resisting and fighting back. At times the anguish might best be released with a piercing scream and tears of anguished sobs. Soon the mind slowly floats into a vapid zone of despair. Soon the memory cells open the flood gates of emotional tears. It's best to let the tears of anguish flow freely. It's best to let the emotional pain release itself from the body. Only then is there relief.

Often the death of someone close causes one to recall past events with the deceased. There are personal and private moments. There are pleasant times. There are likewise humourous incidents. There are even sad events. Sometimes, in the process, the mind would stray. Imagination lends itself to convoluted scenarios of what could have been. There would be endings more joyous than what really happened.

If only the outcome could have been like that. If only it was so. The thought may cause pangs of remorse. There even might be guilty feelings. There is now no chance of parole. In such moments one often forgets that everyone makes many personal decisions without thinking. They might do what seems best at the spur of the moment. They might act without knowing all the facts. They might take action without thinking of all the possible consequences, until it is too late, leaving no other choice but the actual event that happened. Whatever that may be it is now impossible to change. That fact is what one must now accept, no two ways about it. So one has no choice but to treat any memory flashbacks as a historical perspective, to do now what one can to make amends for what cannot be undone. And that's what many do in an effort to move on. To continue moping will not undo what's done. It's now time to move on.

With the passage of time the pain of grief commonly diminishes. Hopefully, it lessens with each memory flash. Overcoming this pain is never easy. Some never let loose these pangs no matter what. At times a stab of distress may open up an inner anger and rage that seems to feed on itself. Moving beyond such an emotional scar will need a change in one's attitude. It takes a conscious effort for one to place the dearly departed within one's personal pages of the past. Now the departed becomes a historical footnote. Now one has to accept that the dearly departed will not be around anymore except in spirit and thought. It is now time to move on. For time waits for no one as it marches forward. Moreover, as time marches on change is inevitable. Things, people and circumstances are all going to change, sooner or later, sometimes ever so slowly, sometimes with a bang. Such changes will very likely create new challenges for those around, challenges which will likely require, periodically, much of one's time, mind and energy. It is therefore foolish to remain engulfed in despair and foreboding, likewise to ponder about undoing what had happened. Such contemplation is wishful thinking. Now one must move on. By moving on, closure usually takes place. Many feel, however, that closure must be done on their terms, must be at their call. Alas, regardless of what one elects to do the universe is going to unfold in a manner beyond one's control, whether one likes it or not. For the universe does not revolve around any single individual. Rather, the universe unfolds in a sequence and order of its own accord. Closure commonly comes with accepting these natural sequences and consequences. Closure is easier to achieve by resolving to try and live a life free of regrets, such as living a life filled with love. One ought to live lovingly with the immediate family, close friends and acquaintances. At the same time one ought to show consideration and care for others. More importantly, a love for life is one way to bring closure to the grieving for another. May there be peace and love in your life as well as your future.

# Growing Up - The Maturing Phase

Maturity is a process which each of us undergoes in a unique way. It takes time, patience and self-actualization. The path to maturity is strewn with trials and errors. There are encountered many differing but oft-repeated challenges to a show of tolerance and consideration for others. These are noted on the following pages. As many readers will find, however, not every paragraph is relevant to their situation. A prior scan of the topical captions might assist in deciding what is appropriate. One aspect to maturity that can be frustrating is to display responsibility by getting a task done. Often what seems easy to do turns out to be a chore. The tasks might progress by fits and starts. Having a game plan which flexes with the situation at hand helps. This is the focus of the closing topic GETTING THE JOB DONE.

## ABOUT BEING RESPONSIBLE

*mere wishful thinking*
*facing the demons within*
*the thought of changing*

An answer has its beginning in a question. Similarly, wanting to change begins with something which we want to change. It could be a nasty personal habit, such as frowning whenever someone asks a question. Or it might be an unsettling way in our character, such as raising our voice whenever we speak to someone although we are next to them. In other words, there is something in one's character one want to change **from**. What has to be determined is what we want to change **to**. So wanting to change for the better encompasses more than a wish, although, many times, wanting to change begins with wishful thinking. Such as wishing for a suasive skill which is not in our present repertoire. But to bring about this change takes more than wishful thinking. We must take a closer look at the character we should know best. Namely, ourselves. This inward introspection should be as realistic as possible. Of course, we ought to avoid flattery and self praise. That might start with trying to understand why we do things the way it's done. It is about understanding our various habits and quirky ways, why sometimes things are done without rhyme or reason. It is about why, on a given day, we may be gentle and kind like a good doctor, such as Doctor Jekyll. Then, on another day, we may become mean and selfish. It is not unlike a terror, like Mister Hyde. Wanting to change starts with a willingness to do so. That, however, is easier said than done. The challenge is to make this wishful thinking a reality. The challenge begins with looking inward at our behaviour. We have to identify, for example, particular habits which upset others. This challenge and subsequent change likely will take more than overnight in effort.

In most circumstances there readily comes to mind just one apt answer to a given question. This happens although there may be many, often different, even contradictory, answers. This plurality of possibilities also applies to most decision we make each day. Nevertheless a person tends to lapse into an answer that reflects her/his set characteristic ways. This is done likely out of personal comfort. These habitual patterns constitute one's personality - habits that, naturally, tend to be self-serving. A few of these habits might be irksome to some. They might be so irksome that a few will react in a negative manner. This reaction, in turn, could trigger our temperamental buttons - buttons that, once pushed, might unleash the demons within. Such demons often emerge in a nasty streak vengeful and with ill will. It is this natural tendency in one's personality that needs a closer look. In each of us there are shortcomings and faults. As for faults, we easily see these in others but not in ourselves. It is now the time to admit having personal faults as well. Otherwise the inner rage will likely raise its ugly head time and again. In the process we will likely once more override logic and courtesy. Putting a check to that rage necessitates that one takes a closer look at one's personality. It implies one has to overcome a personal denial to having any faults. As for having faults let it be said that no one is perfect. In the process of looking inwards the demons are very likely discerned. This is the first step towards confronting them. What has now been achieved is recognizing, maybe faintly, the faults in our personality. The next step is to pursue a remedial action. Once the demons are acknowledged one has to find a way to exorcise the beasts. Incidentally, demons are easily recognizable by the fact that the emotions swell within whenever a person stirs them into action. Of course, not every emotional outburst is a demonic moment. Common sense easily tells the difference.

Changing one's ways, in a willing manner, starts with a fervent desire - a desire filled with a vision of what might be. With this vision there will be many *"what if"* scenarios. This, hopefully, creates a craving within to change. A spark of inner fervour commonly kindles a fickle flame that, unfortunately, can be snuffed out easily once one's thoughts dwell on what must be done to bring about change. Pity. One must kindle and stoke this spark to initiate change, a spark which is capable of setting ablaze the will to change. With the help, of course, of some inner fuel it can happen. And where, pray tell, is that secured ? Why, it is secured from no other place but the mind. For just like the body squeezes energy from food so does the mind feed on energy gained from conscious thoughts. The energy comes from thoughts filled with emotional passion stirring within. This may seem far fetched but it is pretty close to the truth. Just think, for a moment, about someone obsessed with hate. What keeps them so hyped ? Why, just the thought is sufficient. A thought filled with hatred that injects adrenaline through the veins, which creates power surges seemingly throughout the body. So all one needs to do is to take the spark and stoke the emotional passion to create the will to change. Then once the energy starts to rush through the veins it becomes thereafter a matter of consciously focusing the mind on the will to change. It is a matter of funneling the mental energy onto the upcoming phases. It is an episode of mind over matter. Now is the moment for a conscious effort to stoke the determination and will to change.

## TRYING ONE'S BEST

*a contented mind*
*taking charge*
*better late than never*

Not too long ago most people working kept a nine-to-five daily routine. This was an orderly schedule from Mondays to Fridays with appropriate personal time off. Now it's a chaotic scenario. People now work every day of the week, every hour of the day and even all hours of the night; namely, a 24-7 cycle. A similar shift has occurred in the marketplace. For instance, the bread on the grocer's shelf once was white or brown, milk or sandwich; usually sliced. Now it's like the colours of the rainbow : white, wholewheat, rye, pumpernickel, kaiser, baguette and much more. Much the same can be said of clothes, cars or a thousand other items. Choices are many. There are wants for this, demands for that and desires for whatnots. The appetite of the crowd seems to be for novelty and show rather than for survival. The focus seems to be on the social image rather than an ethical or even a spiritual value. For many there is no longer an attempt to strike a balance in the eyes of the public. Ignored in these pursuits is that such possessions likely bring only short-lived pleasure and joy. What seems to be of secondary importance is contentment. Well, believe it or not, there are some contented people around who care less about their possessions and social image. As a matter of fact they appear resigned to their lot in life. They try to make the best of it with what little they have. Such individuals can be found in the poor ghettos of society. Such contentment shows that happiness comes from a state of mind rather than a materially oriented lifestyle. This is the kind of mind-set which helps one to be truly happy. It is a mind-set which underlines that possessing the best possible is not important. Should one be able to afford the best, then by all means possess it. But it isn't going to buy contentment.

It takes more than wishful thinking for one to try their best. There also has to be commitment, zeal and a conscious effort. This includes a willingness to go that extra mile. Naturally, there also has to be a realistic plan as well as a clear goal and purpose. Should one be working alone then the tempo of effort, breaks and rest are easily determined. But in a joint effort involving others these factors need to mesh with the overall schedule as to what is to be done and by when. So, at times, it might be a waiting game. There might also be moments when one is filled with enthusiasm so brimming one might decide to make things happen. The intensity of the moment may propel a person into action. The result is that one is able to get done their allotted tasks and more. However this zealous effort might not be appreciated by others on the team. Sometimes they view one's action as a ploy with an ulterior motive. A few might ascribe this motive to wanting to take charge and doing things one's way. There could be unintended crossed purposes during execution. So doing more than one's quota, in a joint effort can have an unintended ripple effect on one's motive. What should have been done is to communicate one's intention, beforehand, to those affected. That process only ends when there is a meeting of the minds on who does what. Without such consensus there is likely going to be a strain on the working relationship. It may surprise a few as to who would view one's zealous effort in a negative light. Well, such individuals are likely to be none other than those within the extended family, intimate friends or business associates. On the other hand the power of effective communication ought not to be ignored. By communicating effectively one's intended effort and then getting consensus there likely will be generated good will and bonding to one's benefit.

Living in today's society commonly means getting involved with other people. One aspect to the success of such relationships, which some neglectfully don't do, is getting along. Getting along may mean compromising one's customary way of doing things. Getting along may mean talking and conversing about trivia and current affairs. Unfortunately, quite a few are unwilling or uncomfortable about making such an effort. Their attitude seems to be one of not wanting to show any intimacy, as if they do not want others to know any faults or flaws in their character, as if they don't have any. What such individuals fail to see is the symbiotic effect of camaraderie. By merely being friendly and open one can boost the morale of the group. In turn, such morale tends to make the joint effort achieve success with ease. What such individuals fail to realize is that getting along does not mean baring one's soul and home to others. What it means is a spirit of friendship to foster consensual co-operation. Finally, what such individuals fail to see is that effective communication comes through talking and conversing whereby commonly used words and phrases, bantered around in the group, may take on a meaning new to one's vocabulary. Nonetheless quite a few shy away from getting along by just refusing to take the first step of making small talk. The challenge to these individuals is to break out of their familiar comfort of inhibition and start talking. It's better late than never to start doing so.

## SHADES OF GRAY

*differing opinions*
*for the better or for the worse*
*more ways than one*

Civility seemingly adheres to a set of mostly unwritten rules of a community. A set of code that often is just taken for granted within that social sphere. For example, a person would not punch someone else for no apparent reason. Likewise it is customary for one to interact with respect no matter who the party might be. But what about a situation whereby a teasing pinch is put on the cheeks of someone's bum ? The pinchee may react in a variety of ways such as in amusement or maybe total outrage. Should this remain a private matter between pincher and pinchee ? How others view the pinching incident will very likely vary. These different shades of opinions just go to show how a simple incident can be interpreted so differently. Once upon a time such an episode would be considered outrageous. But in today's setting such a common civil outlook is not as strong in outrage. Furthermore, now civility has to extend beyond one's immediate society. In today's society civility now embraces a global village of social values. There is now an added dimension as to what one may think is appropriate. Now one has to hesitate about an opinion on social behaviour until other incidents reinforce one's point of view. For the varied social values now have roots in many differing cultures as well as the related behaviours. In all instances what likely matters most is to observe tolerance and respect.

As each of us goes through life we witness change. Change happens everywhere. Change is a constant of the universe whether in nature or a man made environment. Sometimes change comes at a slow pace like the aging process. Sometimes it's abrupt like an accident. Change creates new situations and circumstances. Change can be as irreversible as time. Now what counts is the present moment. Change also happens in people. For example, consider what happens whenever one runs into someone they haven't seen for quite a while. Part of the conversation usually drifts into any personal change of the other party. A common comment is about how age has not changed them one bit. What is also noticed, but not mentioned, is any change to their personality different from that embedded in one's memory, maybe, for example, about how fate has made them more reticent and looking older than they are. Ah well, people change with the unfolding circumstances and events in their individual life. Funny how one tends to bypass, in their mind, the most important individual that is changing. It is, namely, oneself. Just like everything else in the universe, one's characteristic traits and ways also changed with time. If it's not for the better, then it is for the worse. Hopefully, it is for the better.

There is always something new for one to learn. Once learnt one acquires confidence as they repeat the process over and over. Not only that but one tends to add their own personal flavour to the mix. The result is that they eventually develop their own personal way. To that individual this method is tried and true. Often they become seemingly somewhat oblivious to any other way. Here is a story, a true one, to illustrate that point. It is about a husband wanting to help out, after supper, by doing the dishes. This seems to be a simple task. Until he tied the apron on and touched the dishes. That's when the wife laid down the law: the dishes were to be soaped in a certain procedure, rinsed another set way, and dried in a certain proper fashion. Yet people do dishes every which way. Each day these various ways are done all over the world. And practically all these dishes are good and clean. So how the dishes were done was not really the issue. Could be that the wife wanted to ensure a personal level of comfort. Could more likely be that she wanted the husband to listen and to obey. Who knows, she might wish, subconsciously, to be in control. It seems to be the case involving a situation whereby a person is capable of doing a job and is left alone to do so, only to be told that certain parts of the work would be done by someone else. That smacks of an unnecessary constraint just to show who is in charge. This troublesome behaviour can be tested by asking why things must be done in a certain set way. Should the reply lack rhyme and reason then the likely real reason is control. A typical nonsensical excuse is *no reason just company policy.* Another such excuse is *just do as told.* Often the natural reaction to such excuses is sheer sarcasm and perchance childish behaviour.

## TAKING CONTROL

> *the consequences one faces*
> *people to see, places to go*
> *putting it in writing*

Many times one sees, in passing, a situation happening for which they have a ready made answer, until they get to know the facts. For many times the solution might not be as simple as it may seem. Once one understands the ins and outs of the many possibilities then the complexity likely becomes evident. Such complexity is what many seem to face whenever there is a personal dilemma. The solutions possible seem so many that some are hesitant to resolve the problem, as if they are waiting for a perfect answer to flash across their mind. But whatever is decided there likely will be drawbacks, advantages and disadvantages. Rarely is there a win, win, win solution. Still the situation likely begs for a decision. Many, however, seem to prefer, without thinking, not to do anything. That hardly helps. Meanwhile precious and opportune moments are drifting by. So one ought to give a momentary thought to what seems best and just do it. Naturally, should there be time for a second opinion then do seek it. But many times the best solution is one's hunch and gut feeling. One needs to keep in mind, however, that others might not like what one has done. Sometimes they want a resolution which is in their favour. So once action is taken a thought should be given to what others might say about what was done. Keep in mind that they are looking at the situation in hindsight. As such they very likely can see the drawbacks and limitations of one's action. So one ought to be prepared for disparaging remarks and even retaliatory measures. Furthermore, one should admit that a mistake might have been made, should it turn out to be so. As for any future actions one is now in a position to do better, for sure, next time.

During a stressful situation it is natural for one, not liking the moment at hand, to wish that they didn't have a care in the world. A wish, unfortunately, which is more a fantasy than reality. Some way or the other the situation usually gets resolved; for the better or for the worse. Incidentally, the longer the situation continues the more likely the outcome will be for the worse. Eventually in most cases, somehow or the other, the stress fades. Soon thereafter one's pattern of activities lapses into a routine of sorts. Soon there is no hysteria, just day to day trivia. Sometimes there are now slivers of momentary carefree bliss. Sometimes there are moments of having a full stomach and having all ordinary desires met. In a sense one could be accused, at such moments, of having it too good. There might even be a sense of complacency. Even boredom. What to do with one's spare time ? What many would do is to seek out something new and exciting to do. Maybe they seek something thrilling with a pulsating rush. Such contented moments, no matter how brief, could be put, if one so wishes, to constructive use. Such spare moments could be spent to sort out and schedule one's many personal activities: things to do, people to see, places to go. For the mind now is clear and can think straight. Here is a chance for one to size up a potential crisis and to take steps not to let it get out of hand. Here is a chance to resolve any issues before it is too late for damage control. This is one way to avoid creating unnecessary stress often expressed with an emotional outburst - *Ratz, I forgot all about this*. Here is a chance to prevent a sorrowful situation. By taking such steps it is now possible to reach a contemplative state much akin to peace of mind.

Getting organized, for many, seems an irresolvable dilemma. What such individuals should realize, even empathize with, is that everyone faces a similar dilemma. Such as where to start. For as one dwells on this idea, on where to start, all sorts of pressing problems readily come to mind. Especially there loom on one's brow situations that should have been taken care of yesterday. These worrisome thoughts often cause anxiety and an overwhelming impulse to act right away. But another day, at this stage, would probably not make much of a difference. What's more important is the momentary frame of mind to act constructively. It is for one to try and put the outstanding issues into a semblance of order. All one now needs are pen and paper. These are for jotting down the items to do as they come to mind. Usually they come to the conscious mind haphazardly and at random. Incidentally, by scribbling these items into visible words and concrete form there shimmers a ray of hope of possibly getting the situations resolved. Alas, instead of scribbling many seem to prefer pondering remorsefully rather than doing anything else. Often they lean on the emotional guilt, of having done nothing, as a mental crutch, as if fate has already decide what is going to happen. Probably they do not want logically to see that nothing gets done without time and effort - time which one must make, effort which one must give. Otherwise an intention, much less a hope, cannot become a reality. Here is where writing is the key which unlocks that hope.

## GETTING THE JOB DONE

*making the dream a reality*
*glitches are to be expected*
*the end within reach*

More often than not a project begins with merely a bright idea, an idea that grew as the potential takes vision. There might also be visions of what could be as well as of glory. Such visionary insight helps to formulate the steps necessary to get the job done. These steps become the milestones to be reached. Once the first few steps are taken progress may seem to be rampant. Things go clickety click. A quick finish seems possible - until the first glitch. Usually something out of the blue deters progress. The vision may now become cloudy and hazy. Other glitches appear. Things are now changing from seemingly quick success to day-to-day trivia. Situations that were glossed over at the start are being discerned with an ugly undertone. Discouragement might set in. It's important now to regroup. It's time to rethink the dream. This is where many may falter. They are reluctant to reset the buttons. They don't want to adjust the game plan to fit the circumstances being encountered. Often they might now begin to abandon the high hopes that spurred the project. In hindsight they will likely reminisce, later in years to come, about the opportunities lost. There will be thoughts about the chances one had let slip away. About giving up on a vision that could have been. Their pipe dream had vaporized. A dream someone else likely made a reality.

Whenever one works on a venture there, inevitably, are times when circumstances seem to go against every effort exerted. Most times such setbacks are accepted without malice. Adjustments are made and the project moves on. Not so, however, should the setback be caused by others whether knowingly or inadvertently. Many times it is taken personally. There is an urge to get even, although it may mean putting the project aside and on hold, so that one now can focus emotionally her/his energy on retaliating. There might even be a desire to exact vengeance. One now is going astray and sauntering down a chaotic path where likely nothing good will happen. What one needs to do, right from the start, is to realize that glitches will happen, whether these happen by circumstances or by interfering individuals. It is a matter of adjusting to these glitches and moving on, if one so decides, should one wants to stay in control. This involves, when a glitch creeps in, stepping back and taking another look at the big picture: to evaluate and, if necessary, change the game plan accordingly; to check with others on the team about how realistic the upcoming milestones are; to once more share the dream; to listen and incorporate their feedback; to consider that what can go wrong will likely, at this stage, go wrong; to once more make the team alive with a renewed vision; to reach for that brass ring on the carousel of life.

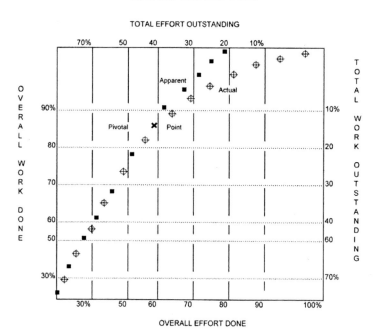

**GETTING THE JOB DONE**

TOTAL EFFORT OUTSTANDING

⊕   the **actual** rate of progress as the project unfolds.

■   the **apparent** rate of progress possible

✖   Beyond the **Pivotal Point** is where effort seems to bring diminishing returns and results. Where the hopes of many seem to flicker and fade. Where determination separates success from failure.

The graph is based on a generalization noted in the "Age of Discontinuity" by Peter Drucker.

At the beginning of a project the end product is a mere figment in the creator's mind. The product is more imagined than real. Sometimes the creator paints a picture of what is to come. With constant effort the concept takes concrete forms. There are now colours. There will then be hard configurations. Even curves evolve. Now and then the form taking shape brings about a reality check. Now one may discern possible limitations. Now one can see noticeable shortcomings. Adjustments more than likely are in order. As the project end nears, however, progress seems excruciating. Sheer persistence and perseverance are now in order. Many wonder why. Well, that's due to the make-up of human nature. At the start the kinetics of the concept and the visions are powerful. The newness and the novelty fuel the urge to get things done. The project is up and running beautifully. Then limitations and shortcomings creep in. Progress seems to get bogged down in details. Still, the urge to continue spurs the process. But inertia already has taken root, as if for three steps forward there are two steps backwards. Setbacks may have dampened the spirit. For the curious these progressive stages are shown, graphically, in GETTING THE JOB DONE. [The graph is based on a generalization noted in 'the age of discontinuity' by Peter Drucker]. During the early stages the project is filled with emotional fervour. The apparent rate of progress is pretty close to the actual - until the pivotal point is reached. After this point many lose heart and courage. They somehow lose the will and the drive to continue at one point or another. Incidentally, at the pivotal point the work is about 85% complete. That's the good news. The bad news is that nearly 40% of the *overall* total effort is now needed to finish. In other words, almost the same amount of effort already spent will now be needed to complete the project. From this point onward any effort made follows the natural law of diminishing returns. So, for example, the last five percent of the work to be done probably needs fifteen percent of the total effort. This is where sheer guts are needed to finish the job. Once done there is a sigh of relief, also a moment of pride and accomplishment. Success has been reached. Success has made all this effort a source of positive personal growth, a glory no-one can take away.

# The Primal Self

Whenever one decides to change usually it is for the better. Often, however, the effort hardly lasts long. There are primal forces within that resist any shift in personal habits without a conscious effort. What it likely will take to change effectively is an understanding of the primal forces underlying our emotions. Within each individual there resides instincts commonly referred to as the seven deadly sins. These have an emotional impact on whatever we do. How each influences our decisions is the focus of the section. I suggest that you pursue, after reading a paragraph or so, an in-depth reflective moment on the topic.

## LOVE OF SELF

*first and foremost*
*a sense for survival*
*listening to one's heart*

One of the strongest bonds of friendship is that of love. It bonds invisibly and emotionally. Love can, at times, makes one forget the weariness of fatigue. Even the passage of time is not noticed. Many have tried putting this into words without much success. For love transcends mere words. Love can, at times, be a driving force to achieve unselfish deeds. Love can also make one risk personal safety no matter how overwhelming the odds. Amazingly, love is ever present within the beat of the heart from one day to the next. This love is so real it is taken for granted, even by yours truly, until one day my wife changed my understanding of this reality. That's when I told her, as I did so many times before, that I love her, in a teasing way. To that she replied that I love myself first. That reply was, for me, an eye opener. For no truer statement can be said. To care for another you have to care for yourself first. So the first and foremost object of your affection has to be yourself. Only then might you be able to love another. This love of self is both instinctive and natural. This love of self is shown in the actions of all. It is self-love that makes us not want to share with others. This self-love motivates the action of a child towards a baby brother, or sister, newly arrived. At the appropriate moment the child would, inadvertently, try to harm the new arrival. The child does not want to share the affection and love once shown solely to her/him by the immediate family. It is self love that impels the actions of people during a war-created upheaval when they are unwilling to share food and clothing. For the love of self is also a survival instinct. A love which is self-centered, natural and passionate.

The flair for staying alive is automatic and natural in everyone. Each has an instinct to do what's necessary to survive. Everyone knows what to do to stay in one piece. This is a built-in propensity to keep body and soul together. One's well being is aided and abetted by the senses. Whenever one recoils from an object too hot it is the sense of touch which is the saving grace. Whenever one spits out a funny tasting morsel it is the sense of taste which emits a warning note. But such natural inclination, however, can be overruled by a more powerful force within one's being. This force is the mind. It is the mind which collects and collates the data and information gained through the senses; the visual panorama of sights, the sighs and sounds echoing in the ears, the sensuous feel and touch of the fingers, the tantalizing tastes on the tip of the tongue, the aromatic scents detected within the nose. These varied sensuous experiences all are stored in the memory cells of the mind. Anything new and strange is examined and scrutinized for future reference. All data and information collected goes into the makeup which includes one's self-preservation instinct. In this regard we each have a mind of our own, a mind which then reacts to circumstances instinctively for self-preservation. The flair for self-preservation can best be seen in the initial natural reaction of young children. Their first impulse is to be selfish, until they learn to behave otherwise. It is this secondary interpersonal reaction which is being dictated by the developing mind.

There are times we wish to be alone. We want to be by our lonesome self. There could be a hope for a moment of respite. The least of one's desires at that moment is to interact with others. But that wish sometimes would be easier said than done. Such solitary desire commonly happens amid a crowd of people. They may be family or they may be friends. They could be fellow workers or perhaps clients and customers, even total strangers. To make matters awkward one might be in no mood for casual conversation. Worse yet should the mood be nasty in the party with whom one is dealing - a downright challenging situation. Now is not the time to lose one's cool. Rather logic needs to prevail. Even if one is far from being calm and collected. One now needs to draw upon that inner reserve. One now needs to employ an intuitive fervour for tranquility. What one needs to do is to slow down and to listen inwardly. It is time to listen to one's heart. The heart is the source of inner peace when called upon consciously. The heart's pulsing beat can banish the mood of misery because the heart is the source of wellness in the human spirit.

## ONE'S EMOTIONAL MAKE UP

> *it shows*
> *emotional pitfall*
> *creature of habits*

Uncontrollable, spontaneous and impetuous. That's usually how one's emotion gushes forth, sooner or later, no matter how hard a person may try not to let it. For it's tough to lock one's emotions into a box and hold firmly to the key. Moreover it's just so hard to tell which situations or what circumstances would trigger an emotional reaction. It may well be a riveting glance, a glance which may create a spark of inner joy, a joy which might give a new meaning to life. On the other hand it could be a glance seemingly filled with sarcasm and hate. This might cause a verbal response filled with unprintable expletives. Such are the varied, and many, responses of the emotions. The challenge is to keep the emotions somehow in check. To do so one should pursue an understanding of human nature. One needs to perceive the individuality in people. That takes a realization that no two people are exactly alike. A set of people may have a lot in common but, nonetheless, have individual differences one from the other. Likewise one ought to realize that others do things sometimes quite differently from the way one may prefer. How one reacts to such irksome scenarios often shows up emotionally. And it is difficult to hide, whether it be disappointment or delight. The challenge is not to let the emotions sway one's decision on what to do. Otherwise the other party may respond in like manner. This might lead to a forceful exchange whether verbal or physical. Before long there likely is a sequence of events escalating out of control. And control is what one ought to seek and wish for: control which commonly comes whenever things are done in a calm and collected manner; control which usually presupposes that things would be done in a rational and logical fashion. That should be one's desire.

In any given situation many would, if free to do so, choose the easy way out. One such easy decision is not to get involved in others' causes. Similarly many prefer, in their daily routine, to follow a pattern familiar, predictable and friendly. Any dissension shown to others would likely be of a token nature, so that, this way, their personal agenda may stay on track. But many times that is not to be. Circumstances and others may get in the way. The result is anxiety. How one reacts would vary from one person to the next. A few may sulk and mumble. A possible sign of that reaction is that they become fidgety. Usually they would check, often in a nervous and constant fashion, for any change to the status quo. Others believe third parties would intervene in one's favour. Sometimes they do. Sometimes they don't. Then there are those who let things come to a boil. In the process they are frustrated. And then they explode emotionally. What usually follows are verbal accusations and abuse. Sometimes this leads to an escalating confrontation. What most fail to understand is that their opening personal actions likely created the deteriorating situation and subsequent outcome. To keep one's cool no matter how much others try to rattle their cage ought to be the first and foremost objective. To avoid such emotional pitfalls must be one's personal goal. To do this one has to think above and beyond a self-centered agenda. To do this one needs to have an insight as to the many faces of the varied emotional forces. That will take time and patience. Ironically, it is time and patience which need to be shown, at all times, in the first place.

Long before the mind etches its first logical thought the emotions are up and running. The first action is the wail of a new born as they put air and oxygen into the lungs. Shortly thereafter come the wails and cries for differing needs: a mother's milk, the discomfort of a dirty diaper, the psychological warmth of a parental hugging hold. But a more important wail of a tiny tot is a plea for attention. How a child learns to control their plea is as individual as can be. Quite a few would get their own way otherwise there will be a temper tantrum. But some learn that wailing doesn't help one bit. Most use their common sense to plea for just a wee bit. If there is no response then they resign themselves to the situation. Once attention is given then there is now time for cooing, smiling and bonding. What comes next in the growth stage is the child learning how to communicate as well as how to interact with others. This they, naturally, learn from the immediate elders nearby. In the process also transmitted are the emotional overtones for the relevant phrases and language. Unfortunately many times children adopt any related bias even though their common sense may tell them otherwise. With repetition, however, the bias is believed. Likewise passed on are the ethnic traditions and family customs which become part of the child's eventual behavioural pattern. At the same time each child develops her/his own individual style which, over time, becomes a habit. So accustomed, after a while, would children be to this routine that they are creatures of habits. Needless to say, such a protocol continues into one's adult life. Thus the emotions are intimately interwoven into one's personality and ways. To each there is a unique set of emotional references for language which one ought to keep in mind. In other words, a certain expression, phrase or word may seem harmless, as far as one is concerned, but there might be an emotional overtone to another individual. To illustrate this dimension just mention *"rass"* to a Jamaican you may know and observe the response.

# THE DEADLY EMOTIONAL SINS

*self-centered ways*
*the demons within*

Emotions. These are primal forces. These are volatile and tumultuous traits. They can, in a flash, run amok over any well thought out logical stratagem. Controlling the emotions is not easy. Often in making a decision there is an emotional element included. Likewise, many times the emotions add another dimension to the spoken words. For example, one can understandably empathize with the sobbing plea of someone hurt or the hysterics of a person upset. Or one can sense the magic of a charismatic speaker. But there is also a dark side to the emotions. The emotions are capable of driving a person to psychiatric frenzy. The impact might lead to paranoid behaviour. Often, for many, there are created foibles, indecisiveness and troublesome thoughts. There may even be psychoses and neuroses. Still, quite a few are able to suppress the pulls and eddies of the emotions. What these individuals do is to just focus on their own personal welfare and interest. This is easily done because the natural instinctive priority of everyone is to keep mind and body together with a self-centered passion, even if this is done, inadvertently, at the expense of others. Such a trait often is observed in the actions of many.

Once upon a time in an ancient epoch, long before the common era, the keeping of mind and body together was a full-time occupation. There were no cultivated fields anywhere to harvest. There were no livestock of cows or pigs in a pen. People were surrounded by just nature and the wild. Everywhere were predators and scavenging animals including humans. Kill or be killed was the order of the day. People had to rely, full-time, on their survival instincts and skills to stay alive. With the passage of the ages a civilized society eventually emerged, a society where most people strive to co-exist with each other. Law and order now became the norm. The survival instincts, once primary and necessary, now seem to be relegated to a dormant role. Though not quite so, for the survival instincts now serve a role in many self-centered personal agendums. Whenever activated the instincts seem to make a person somewhat insensitive to the needs of others. The identification of these instincts ought to be attempted. It seems this was done, indirectly and unbeknownst, in the middle ages when certain individuals cloistered themselves in splendid isolation. Such an isolation was practised by the early Christians wholeheartedly in a monastic life. Such an isolation produced the inmost desires and wants within. As defined by Pope Gregory the Great, it was *a classification of the normal perils of the soul in the ordinary conditions of life*. To me this classification likewise defined the natural instincts that come into play, as need be, for survival including the survival of the human species. In any event the classification is the cause, for sure, of many a guilty conscience. The classification described traits which Thomas Aquinas, a philosophical saint, defined as the seven deadly sins. *Vainglory* or vanity and pride. *Covetousness* or greed. *Lust*. *Envy*. *Gluttony* or Overindulgence. *Anger*. *Sloth* or laziness. They are deadly not because these natural traits are malicious by themselves; rather, because they tend to be a proclivity for more grievous offenses, like murder, creating, through obsessive thoughts, personal pursuits which seem to take on a life of their own. They take shapes and forms in the guise of personal demons within the mind. Yet they all can be easily identifiable in people we know. Better yet the fault people find in others is most likely the very one deadly within their own self. Not recognizing this aspect of fault-finding is the deadliest aspect of it all.

## VANITY

> *seeing is believing*
> *wanting to be seen favourably*
> *dizzy in the head*

Upon seeing someone familiar one usually can recall the first impression that person made. That tells how powerful an initial image is. That's why many try to be appropriately attired and groomed as the occasion demands. They know that image counts. How far an individual may pursue this issue, however, is a personal call. Quite a few, for instance, exercise and diet to ensure a lean and trim figure stays in view. Others may go as far as employing cosmetic surgery. It's all a telling aspect to modern day narcissism. Still, to look attractive, even glamourous, is an asset. It's easier for one to relate and interact with an individual who is properly groomed and attired. Moreover, to be vain, in that respect, has its purpose in nature as well as in the animal kingdom. That's why a majestic lion struts his stuff, why a peacock spreads its plume - namely, it certainly helps to attract a mate. The purpose is all about sex appeal and an inviting tease to possible intimacy. Sometimes there is a need to utilize an alluring scent, perhaps a hoot and even a howl, just to catch the eye of another they desire. That's the underlying reason why people, knowingly or not, are attentive to personal appearance. But, as many have found out, vanity cannot be pursued endlessly. To do so is as elusive as eternal youth. As the years pass, therefore, the reality check we have to face is that we ought to, willingly, act our age from a psychological point of view.

Vanity and pride, of course, go beyond the physical realm. It is natural, for example, to be proud of what one has or can do. Such pride enhances our self-esteem and confidence, until we encounter someone who has or can do better. When that happens it hurts. Most accept this fact of second fiddle sooner or later. Much the same hurt happens, usually to a lesser degree, whenever one makes a silly mistake or loses an argument or is played for a fool. How one reacts to any such incident is what counts. The first reaction ought to be admitting the error in one's ways. Otherwise one would be in denial and nothing good can come of that. Besides, to make a mistake is a part of our nature. Still there are instances whereby an individual refuses to admit making a mistake. They seem to prefer living a lie. Once such an attitude is adopted then it commonly continues. All this happens on account of a bit of vanity.

As one progresses along the learning curve there are data and protocols new to study. Whenever anything new is learnt there is a natural inclination to try this and test that, in effect, a trial and error phase. After a while we are on our own. Thereafter we have to make decisions for the better or for the worse. There will be successes. There will be failures. Usually most take these in strides. But should there be a string of failures one's self confidence, perchance even self-esteem, may falter. Successive failures tend to create greater self-doubt and maybe an unwillingness to take any risk, stemming from a frustrated feeling of seemingly wasted effort. But failure can be a personal lesson about humility and about making oversights, often unintended. It is a lesson on the selfish aspect to arrogance. On the other hand success followed by subsequent successes might cause individuals to focus narrowly only on their personal agenda and ego. They might therefore limit their vision to a self-centered one. Sometimes this projects a cold hearted individual. Often, however, the individual doesn't realize why or doesn't really care. It is likely, in the opinion of some, a case of success literally going to their heads. But it is likely a case of success making them believe that it is not necessary to change anything in their ways and personal program. Moreover success tends to make them ignore the opinions of others. The more successful some become the more they seem entrenched in their self-centered ways. It could also be that they seem to demand respect and admiration. What they should not overlook, however, is that personal success may well be just a transient personal phase. Nonetheless there are successful people who seemingly try to share their success with others. Hopefully, this will redress any earlier oversights.

> *The contemplative trait overriding vanity is humility. To counteract vanity takes ADMITTING ONE'S MISTAKES as noted in the BEING HUMANE section.*

## GREED

> *wanting this and wanting that*
> *pebbles and scruples*
> *the gilding of the heart*

Every so often we witness an avarice for greed by individuals as they hastily take more than they need. Should it be over food then, to some, it's understandable, for, to them, it shows a natural survival instinct. But greed, of course, goes beyond food. Greed seems to be, for instance, the thrill which feeds a gambler's passion. Moreover, should greed be an instinctive trait then it ought to be evident even in children, including children who are innocent and naive. Children can get worked up over a festive occasion like a birthday party. At such functions they eagerly sing the Happy Birthday refrain then partake of cake, candies and treats. It is, for them, fun and good times. Similarly, at Christmas they unwrap, with glee, the novelty new and playful presents. Just the thought of that could make a kid scribble a wish list an arm and a leg long, wanting this game, coveting that toy. Imagine getting everything they ever wanted. It would engulf their room at home. There likely wouldn't be enough time and hours to enjoy it all. Such is the dilemma with someone possessed with avarice. They want to hoard for no apparent reason other than wanting it all. Such is the nature of greed. The tough part is letting go. For some that seems next to impossible.

As we go through life we collect trinkets and mementos, much like a child who saunters, barefoot, along the shorelines picking up pebbles which dazzle their eye, pebbles which, one by one, accumulate into a treasure trove. Such a trove, to the possessor, gives a warm feeling akin to a cozy security blanket. The older one gets the more fanciful the pebbles. These could be cars, mansions, objets d'art and gorgeous toys all adorned with bells and whistles. At the same time, around the block, would be those who lack the ways and means to possess such trinkets but they would have the craving. To satisfy this void they, if given the chance, would make off with what they can, even though it's not theirs. That's how some satisfy their greed. Such skullduggery is very much in the minds of pebble owners. To counteract such shenanigans they would take measures such as lock and key plus, if need be, protective electronics. Often what subsequently develops, however, is a subjective suspicion of anyone who may seem to have interest in their pebbles. No matter how innocent or genuine that interest may be it is considered to be hostile. As a consequence quite a few might develop a fortress mentality. Over time, however, this could coalesce into a denigrating attitude towards certain social groups. Such a negative opinion usually becomes part of the social landscape. The sad aspect is that many, who are affected by such negative attitudes, could not care less about the pebbles in question.

Ashes to ashes. Dust to dust. These are the oft repeated phrases of the burial rites of those who died. This includes individuals who have accrued treasures and fortunes. Many, while alive, seemed intent on taking it all with them even beyond the grave. But have no fear, the legacy inevitably would be put to good use by someone else. In turn there will be an epitaph befitting the deceased. The greater the legacy the more monumental would be the epitaph. But gathering the wealth and fortune tells only half the story. The other aspect is the attitude of such people while alive. For often the more they have the more they seem to want. All they gathered would now need to be safeguarded and protected. At the same time having such possessions seems to cause a condescending attitude to those of lesser fortune. They ought to occasionally consider what good would it do should they gain all the treasures of the world. They should also contemplate judging others for who they are rather than for what they have. Most importantly they should strive to deal with everyone they meet from the heart rather than a monetary bottom line.

*The contemplative trait overcoming greed is charity. To counteract greed there is a need to HAVE A HEART as noted in the BEING HUMANE section.*

## LUST

*the source for human life*
*more than a sexual spark*
*wanting control*

Love, attests a fairly recent ballad, makes the world go round. It did then and certainly still does today. What's not said, likely taken for granted, is the underlying lust which powers that drive. Lust provides the necessary spark, the wherewithal, for you and I to be here. When the desire is mutual then joy of joys. But it is not quite the same should one of the parties be an unwilling partner. It is a crime whereby someone imposes her/his will on a reluctant participant. That's the kind of behaviour most associate with lust. Nevertheless there is a little lust in everyone, for lust is a natural cyclical bodily function and process, a process which, believe it or not, provides inner energy and personal drive. Many use such energy and drive to fuel imaginative and physiological actions. Lust may fuel, for instance, day dreaming fantasies of greatness. It likewise helps to focus the mind on gaining knowledge. Personal excellence in the field of sports, for example, needs such drive to persevere with the necessary practice. Each and everyone can tap into this inner source of energy. All it takes is determination and focus. An appropriate use, should one so choose, is to be constructive in one's endeavours. A suggested use, in this respect, is to plan ahead one's activities. By doing so pitfalls are foreseen and appropriate steps taken to get the job done. In turn this allows one to grow in personal self confidence.

Lust, by itself, is a natural physiological drive. It is, of course, an innate animalistic need which ensures propagation of the human species. Once aroused, it is a powerful craving akin to the pressing need of a spoiled brat with a temper tantrum. As overwhelming as this urge may become, however, it is possible to focus beyond the urge. For, unlike air, food and water, it may seem, but is not, an absolute necessity. For it is not needed for a person to stay alive and continue to be in this world. Probably that is why lust is associated with the violent actions of men seemingly deranged. Still, lust beats beneath each human heart. For lust is more than a biological instinct for self-centered satisfaction. Lust also is a subconscious desire for self fulfillment. It is physiological as well as psychological. Thus lust is more than an inner craving for physical union and superficial unity. Lust also is an inner desire for self-love, whether that be momentarily or more sustaining, whether that be a joy of joys or a fantasy of the mind. Lust ignites the will and drive to strive towards such fulfillment. Lust fires the conscious thoughts in such a quest. On the other hand lust can incite a person to want having their own way. Thus, in the process, one can become blind and insensitive to others. In such a pursuit any negative comments by others might be brushed aside with disdain. Any meaningful objection might be blinded by the vision of the fantasy being a reality. The result is a sledgehammer of words to crush opposing viewpoints as well as menacing threats and even physical force. Such is the inner energy which can be generated by means of the lust beating beneath the heart. It is now a matter of putting that energy and drive to constructive, or destructive, use.

In the early years of one's infancy there is no other choice but to depend on parents and guardians, totally and completely, for food and care. This includes stimulation of the brain and senses as part of the natural order. It could be said that the welfare of the child comes first. Such caregiving action leads to an intimate bond between child and parents particularly with the mother. With each passing day this bond grows in intensity and into a loving relationship. In fact often the parents are willing to make personal sacrifices for the sake of the child. Time and time again, it is for the sake of the child. Such loving care leads to wanting no harm to come to the child. This love protects the child from adversity of any kind. Sometimes, however, this loving care persists past infancy and even past puberty. It could be said to be a possible case of over-caring and a matter of over-protection. Unfortunately, this is another form, often subconscious, of lust for control. It is control against a person's will. Such controlling action happens all the time, in many families, without a thought given about the psychological scar. Such parental lust is often justified in the guise of doing good - "For the good of the child" - even though the child in question is old enough to think, and decide, for her or himself thus the control seems unwarranted. Such lust for control, unfortunately, is also common with people in power. Often they exercise such lust without ever consulting, beforehand, the people affected. They do so by declaring that they do so in the best interest of everyone, as if these people can't decide for themselves. In their mind, however, the declared actions are being done in good faith. Such form of control happens all the time. It is a lustful form of power. Naturally, it happens with the best of intentions. And all this lustful power comes from the heart. Heaven help those who are the so called beneficiaries.

> *The contemplative trait controlling LUST is loving kindness. To counteract LUST the focus ought to be giving according to the SWAYS OF THE HEART as noted in the BEING HUMANE section.*

## ENVY

> *going one better*
> *desiring this and coveting that*
> *going beyond wanting*

To grudge what another has is a common phenomenon. It comes about whenever someone else possesses something better. It may be a glitzy possession or a special talent. Whatever it is a person feels an urge within that they must have it or be able to do it just as well. Often such envy is betrayed only in the glint of the eyes. Sometimes the glint is one of admiration but most times it is one of envy. Most times, for most people, the sensation is short lived. They then return their focus and attention to whatever they were doing before. But that glancing moment may awaken an inner desire. There stirred within a pressing desire to call such a possession, or talent, all their own. Sometimes such envy can spur one on to seek out and secure the same item or new skills. Thus envy can be a positive influence. Envy can motivate one to pursue an ambitious path. Envy may push one to try and shine above all others and to rise above the norm. To be able to go to the next level came about because of envy.

Few give much thought to the numerous advantages they presently have. If there is a concern it is likely about what they don't have. For no matter how good they may have it someone else has it better. Many are the items that fit this description: possessions, wit, prestige and social advantages. Funny how one-sided envy can be. Consider, for example, preferential treatment. No problem should one be the individual benefiting. But it could be quite upsetting should the beneficiary be someone else. Such is the delusion of envy and self-importance. What seems to be overlooked, in all of this, is that nothing usually worthwhile and everlasting ever comes from an envious thought being fulfilled, other than ill-will and regrets. Worse yet is that after an envious person gets what they want they usually don't want it.

Envy sometimes goes beyond wanting this and wanting that. Envy can also promote one's self-interest and agenda. As such it also resides within the hearts of those who already have it made. As such they, in their wisdom and judgement, exercise their power and influence for self-interest. Incidentally, at one time envy had no room for self-interest and that was during the era when people spent practically all their waking hours scrounging for food. Desiring these natural titbits and wanting that wild morsel, then, made people mimic the productive ways of the more successful hunters. With food now so readily at hand envy apparently has shifted its focus, for many, onto preserving their self-interest by whatever available means. So being envious is a good sign but in today's world many want this zeal fulfilled at a price others likely must pay. Needless to say, in spite of such hindrances the talented eventually still get there.

> *The contemplative trait banishing envy is respect. This aspect is discussed in HAVING NO RESPECT of the BEING HUMANE section.*

## GLUTTONY

> *overdoing it*
> *a matter of taste*
> *seeking a distraction*
> *going beyond a time portal fantasy*

In many ways the limits of the body are way below the unfettered fantasy of the mind. Take, for example, what one puts in one's mouth. It is not unusual for individuals to keep stuffing themselves even though their now stretched stomach says no more. But this signal is ignored and the intake of food or intoxicating drink continues to flow in. Even hallucinogenic substances are swallowed, a case of the mind wanting to continue the pleasurable sensation over the irksome feeling of the body. So the body tries to adjust, even if this means changing the normal and natural body chemistry. An example is the storing of excess fat beneath the skin. Or it can be the coating of plaque upon the inner arteries. Worse yet is the reprogramming of the cells within the neural cortex to accommodate the incoming abusive substance of exotic chemicals. To change such processes would depend on the personal prerogative of the mind and will. But that is not easy. For what happens is that a wish now has become a want, a want evolving into a taste, a taste leading to a habit, a habit to a need and, finally, a need to a compulsion. To revert back to the original situation would require controlling all these developed mental impulses, which now constitute a part of the individual's way of life, and also have become an integral part of the individual's disposition. Any possible hope for change now totally depends on one's determination. For, as the saying goes, if there is a will there is a way.

In the primeval era people spent most of their time scouting the landscape for something to eat. They searched for food amid the natural vegetation. In that epoch clean sweet spring water flowed. Often they learned, in a tragic way, what was edible and what's not, namely, by tasting. Instinctively they spat out the bad, such as rotten vegetation. But nowadays many seem to focus on food mostly for the pleasure. They wish to explore, for example, the cuisine of exotic dishes. So they savour the exquisite delight of fine wines and liqueurs enhanced, perchance, within an ambient setting. In conducive surroundings many get carried away easily. They then give in to the bodily senses of 'feed me, feed me'. But they continue to indulge beyond the stomach signaling enough. In the process they override common sense and any self control. Alas, excess often happens in many day to day ordinary meals. At such times one ought to practise moderation. A sensible recipe is to end a meal slightly hungry and definitely wanting more. Within a reasonable time thereafter the stomach likely will signal enough. A byproduct of this approach is a sleeker waistline as well as less fat in the bloodstream. A benefit to this approach is less chance of plaque coating the arteries. Bon appétit.

In today's world it is difficult to avoid stress. There is stress at work. There is stress within the home environment. Stress even is felt at a supposedly enjoyable social gathering. Often stress is identified with people. No wonder many try to avoid a crowd. Individuals prefer instead just to be with friends or, better yet, alone. Sometimes, however, the residual stress becomes so gnawing that one desires to do something so as to occupy the mind with something simple and stress free. One such distraction readily at hand is food. Food provides nourishment to the body. Food stimulates the taste buds on the tongue, and inner walls of the cheeks, with each flavour-producing chew. Often this distracting habit starts with a handful of tit-bits. Munch by munch the distraction may continue. Soon this distraction becomes a regularity. Often also at other meals, such as dinner, extra portions are put away mostly for the enjoyment. In the fullness of time such intakes become a way of life. There is now a life with an extra layer of fat. To get rid of such bodily weight is now easier said than done. Resolving to limit one's food intake might be tried with the best of intentions. Such attempts are usually short lived. For the ingrained habit of overindulging often masks an inner turmoil, which kick starts the habit of overindulging, a turmoil that won't easily go away and lurks just below conscious thought. Should denial of this turmoil continue then overindulging will likely continue. Thus there is a crying need to take a deep look inwardly. To try and consciously face this demon festering within the mind. No more denial of the beast within should persist. A beast which brought about the problem of overindulging has taken over. Worse yet, but very much similar in causation, is the habit of drinking to excess. The habit of drinking to excess is so evident when it happens. Not so evident, however, is the turmoil which fueled the drinking to excess.

To fantasize is a common phenomenon. One such common fantasy is to wish a life different from the present. So it is common to wish there somehow be a time portal to a new life. One such destination is to a different place and time in history. The desire seems to be for freedom from the present circumstances and personal baggage. Possibly promising is the ability to undo the errors of their ways, even if they had to promise to walk the walk and talk the talk. Many individuals who overindulge would gladly walk through such a time portal. It would make, for them, a world of difference. But, alas, they really do not have such a choice in the matter. For their overindulgence habit seems etched into their present personal template of behaviour, an etching likely scratched with a futile sense of 'what's the use'. In spite of such an ingrained habit they, now and then, have sparks of determination to mend their ways - until the first emotional setback is met. Then they usually seek the comfort of their overindulging habit of old, thus putting out whatever spark of determination kindled. What they ought to do is to try and transform their personal pattern of behaviour. They should try, for example, to get involved deeply with an unselfish cause, a cause which is meaningful in their eyes such as extending a helping hand to family and friends. Getting involved with such causes often gives a personal sense of purpose. In the process the mould of looking only at their self-centered world would break. Once a sense of self worth, by giving of oneself, is gained then the challenge of foregoing their own overindulging habit might be met. The challenge, once assumed, ought to include eating less and drinking more water plus a personal plan to exercise. This should be real sweaty physical exercise. A program that gets kick-started with just a step, then a walk, regularly, the longer the better. Gradually change to a brisk pace, if possible, a jog. Such an exercise program ought to become an integral part of their lifestyle routine. Life now would have a different pattern and a new meaning. The personal template of before would become a thing of the past, rapidly being layered over with new challenges and circumstances. With such a sense of determination the overindulgence habit now can be shunted through the time portal into the past.

*The contemplative trait conquering GLUTTONY is periodic fasting. To counteract gluttony it takes CURBING THE APPETITES as noted in the BEING HUMANE section.*

## ANGER

*losing it*
*getting no respect*
*keeping one's cool*

How one fares financially commonly sways one's outlook and mood. For instance, with good fortune and prosperity laughter comes easily. Any mistakes and oversights, by others, might be taken with a grain of salt. It's not quite the same, however, for bad times. In such times events seem to unfold counter to one's interest. The tension within is taut. Anger comes easily. The pent-up feeling building within is unleashed by a minor infraction usually unrelated to the cause of the stress. Such anger is common. It is somewhat understandable. Another source of anger is the way children act, consciously or not, towards their parents once the children leave home and are on their own. Almost all parents raise their offspring with tender loving care, unselfishly showering on them attentive devotion mingled with personal sacrifice. In return parents wouldn't mind a show of affectionate appreciation. But what is sometimes shown is seemingly ungrateful behaviour causing a parental hurt. Most anger is a reflection of a similar personal hurt. A hurt often interpreted to be caused by a selfish act, at least in the eyes of the person hurting. Often such expectation differs from what actually happens. Often their expectation is that their concern would be addressed, first and foremost, by others, whether that be for past favours, even personal sacrifices, or other possible reasons real or imagined. Often a show of anger is thus caused by events unfolding contrary to one's expectations. But what usually happens is that people would, instinctively, first consider a course of action which would be in their own best interest. Occasionally there may come to mind the concerns of others which might then be included in the action taken. But often the expectation of the person becoming angry excludes such a possible course of action, almost as if only their agenda counts, as if they are someone whose influence and power is to be respected, if not obeyed. Such a sense of self importance usually is what ignites anger. The resulting outburst is a way of saying that they are a force to be reckoned with. Just wait and see. The seed of vengeance may have been just planted. Sometimes that would, if the relationship continues, lead to an eventual violent confrontation.

There seems to be a lot of anger around these days. Anger that seems to gush out of people unexpectedly out of the blue. Often the cause is not so readily apparent. It usually stems from unfulfilled personal expectations. A common source is disappointment or things not going their way. One cause of anger, believe it or not, is an abiding faith in fair play, a case of tit for tat. Just because one person fulfilled her/his end of the bargain then the other party MUST do the same. Get real. That, sometimes, is wishful thinking. As a result people get angry. But striking back in a rage is a losing effort. There is likely little to be so gained except for a temporary moment of satisfaction. Such rage then may lead to an escalating series of confrontations. Besides an angry outburst will not change the present situation. Maybe one may gain a promise for the other party to fulfill their end of the bargain - a possibly dubious guarantee. Keep in mind also that, no matter how justified one may be, an outward show of rage usually would make anyone nearby keep their distance. Who wants to tangle with a raving maniac ? If anything, they would then likely take the side of the other party. What should one then do ? Stay calm and collected, no matter how difficult that may be. By staying cool one is able to think straight. By doing so one might project an outward decorum for any constructive resolution of the problem. To resolve the situation to one's satisfaction, however, is likely not going to happen. Accepting that possibility is the tough part to the situation. But that's life. Chalk this one up to experience.

It is not possible, at times, for people to pursue peaceful co-existence in a stressful situation or a crowded environment. Once a person's cage is rattled they might be an angry outburst - ranting and raving, often acting unreasonably. Once this steamy moment blows over they usually become regretful, even apologetic. Most can relate to such an outburst. Many somehow are able to get past such a maddening moment without losing their cool, as if they realize that everyone has a will of their own, to thus, should they so decide, do as they damn well please. Hence what another may decide to do could differ from what one may want them to do, no matter the circumstances. Accepting what they may decide to do, however, can be a concern, more so should the choice of action be asinine. Nonetheless they did what they wanted and now it's after the fact. Maybe they did it without thinking. As the saying goes, anyone can make a mistake. But what ended up happening might be to one's detriment, thus upsetting. The challenge one faces is how to get past the resulting maddening moment, more importantly, to keep one's cool. For sure, there should not be uttered a word in anger. Sometimes, by remaining calm, the upsetting party may become contrite and put forward an acceptable solution. Another reason not to get upset is to make sure one is able to think straight. To then come up with a constructive plan of action encompassing one's concerns. Often what some people do is not to get mad but to get even. Others have responded in a non-violent way, namely, passive resistance, a way effectively used by Gandhi and Martin Luther King. No matter what one decides to do next, keep in mind the consequences that will likely take place. Why pursue a losing cause ? Revenge, you say ? If one enjoys fostering ill-will then, by all means, pursue it.

*The contemplative trait vanquishing anger is understanding gained through patience. To counteract anger involves CONFRONTING ANGER as noted in the BEING HUMANE section.*

## SLOTH

*a sluggish behaviour*
*tomorrow syndrome*
*adrenaline free*

In life there are ups and downs such as moments of joy and intervals of sadness. There are also times of boredom, when tasty dishes seem somewhat flat, when expensive gifts and flashy trinkets somehow lose their sparkle. Boredom commonly causes a fixation about there being nothing to do - well, nothing appealing or worthwhile, just a melancholy feeling, a malaise like lack of energy. One may even have a feeling of self pity and apathy. But boredom has its purpose. It seems to be nature's way to rest the body for stressful moments to come. The slothful behaviour induces a restful respite for the body, a calming of the nerves before an impending personal storm. Sloth, however, has a psychological negative effect. It may induce a loathing for one's ordinary routines, even though there may be people to see, or places to go, or things to do. Pressing menial chores to be done, for example, may seem unimportant. Boredom often now urges us to seek something exciting instead, something out of the ordinary, often a subconscious wanting to be the focus of others' affection if not attention, also wanting one's whims and fancy to be fulfilled. Never mind stepping on the toes of others - only one's immediate desires and needs matter. That's the trouble with boredom. It could create a self-centered world with no concern for others.

Nearly all have odd personal chores to do which they put aside for a rainy day, hardly giving them a moment's thought, often until a chore becomes a quandary. Many times, upon contemplating how numerous the tasks are, however, they may become depressed. Just the thought might have created a hovering dark personal cloud. For the tasks may seem more than the time and effort they intend to spend. Where to start ? Just that could be a problem, for there usually are a few items which were supposed to have been done yesterday. Still, they would just start working on whatever first comes to mind or readily at hand. By being constructive and productive the many tasks, one by one, gradually are done. But not everyone would thus get on with the job. A few prefer to linger and dally on only thinking about what to do, dwelling on the imagined difficulty, commonly deciding that it would be best done the next day, tomorrow when they are fresh and energized. When the morrow comes, however, other issues occupy the day. And so the postponement continues. What happens is that they then prefer to harp about such woes rather than just work on them and get it over with. At times whoever may be listening may take heart and offer to help. This ends up in the one crying woes doing less. With such success it's difficult for such an individual to change their postponing ways, worse yet should they be in denial - namely, that they ought to just face the music and get on with the job. Often upon others asking about the issues they, in denial, would tell a lie, giving an apparent valid, though false, reason for the tasks not being done. Any future probing query likely results in another lie which affirms the first lie. And so on.

And so on. A quagmire of lies which could have been averted just by diligent work. Pity. It is better to do something late than never. Better yet one should try to get done what they can each day so that there will be less to do tomorrow.

Everything having life within grows, a growth that causes movement. In one form or another growth continues, whether molecular within or outwardly visible. It is movement caused by the metabolization of matter and energy. Some life forms do so slowly, others relatively rapidly. In that respect people are no different. For some seem to move slowly and others quite rapidly. As if the pace of metabolization varies from one person to the next. This could be why some are morning-oriented in action, while others are afternoon- or evening-oriented. Such differing rates may play havoc in a coordinated effort. For when one person is ready and eager the other party may not be. This might cause a person to form a poor opinion of another. For often people judge others from their own personal outlook of the moment. Thus a morning-oriented person might likely expect others to be morning-oriented too. If they are not then this could lead to a low estimation of them. They may even attribute the trait to laziness. In their rush to judgement they very likely overlook other possible valid causes, such as a temporary stress disorder or even sleep apnea. Furthermore an individual may develop a lazy disposition by someone else constantly catering to them. So they become spoilt. Besides, if others want to do their tasks then why should they bother. Such individuals usually are capable. Like anyone else, they have adrenaline flowing in their veins. Adrenaline which is a catalyst energizing one to be become hyped and ready for action. All it takes is just a tingle of emotion. Then the adrenaline starts to flow. For no one is adrenaline free. Getting someone else to do what one desires has more to do with how to motivate others. And that's a story for another time.

> *The contemplative trait overcoming sloth is to be busy and constructive. To counteract sloth one has to go about TAKING CARE OF BUSINESS as noted in the BEING HUMANE section.*

## BE TOLERANT IN YOUR THINKING

> *not getting enough*
> *out of respect*
> *trying one's best*
> *making one's wish a reality*

From time immemorial people have searched for ways to add a little spice into their humdrum life. Mixing elixirs and concoctions they then ingest with delight. Many times it is to escape boredom. For much the same reason many crave, and seek, various forms of entertainment and excitement, some going as far as wanton drinking and playful debauchery. For quite a few the more illicit the better it is. Also in vogue is the adrenaline high which comes from bootleg drugs, this all being done, in one form or another, as individuals pursue pleasure. To each their own choosing. With time a pursuit may turn habitual. Once the habit becomes incorruptibly ingrained it is tough to shake. What might be too much before might not be enough now. The thrill of pleasure might now take on a life of its own. They descend deeper into decadence. The will to change is reduced to a mere speck. Being well aware of such an outcome has not deterred many from wanting a taste, just to feel what it's like. So it is common to drift into such wishful fantasy, to then sally, consciously, into such forays. How far they saunter is a personal prerogative, and the same for how long they dally. Before starting they ought to be careful about what they wish for because they might get their wish and more. Such excesses may become not enough to satisfy the craving. In this case the worst thing that happened, believe it or not, is that they got what they wished for. In addition, keep in mind that contentment with one's lot in life hinges on tolerating the humdrum day-to-day banality one encounters.

In a civilized society there always are codes of conduct. Some are unwritten. Some are spelled out in clearly stated sentences in social codes which commonly define social ethics or religious rules or civil law and order. People are expected to honour them, more or less. For there are consequences such as social ostracization or civil punishment. The codes usually vary a bit from one community to the next. Often the codes are rooted in ethnic traditions and local yore. To many inhabitants the codes seem so reasonable that, to them, it might as well be universal. Some codes may be so but, in totality, it is not likely thus. In that respect a newly arrived visitor, from afar, may find certain codes to be peculiar or too arbitrary or even too liberal. Indeed, to the locals some codes might be contentious and considered a bit of a nuisance. At times it is too restrictive for their liking. An example is driving within the set speed limits. Still, the codes are meant to promote equality and fairness - supposedly. For there are individuals who seem to be more equal than others. Many are in positions of power, acting, at times, as if they need not observe the codes especially as if they were above the law. Such actions merely underscore the fragile nature of codes. What ought to be kept in mind is that adherence to the codes is a voluntary, if not willing, act. Should people, as a majority, decide to disregard the codes then there would be a breakdown in civility, followed likely by chaos and anarchy. Social civility depends on the codes as well as the willingness of people to observe them. Such willingness arises whenever people deal with each other, whether socially or in business. In that regard it needs to be said that each person has a character all their own, a character with traits others may like or dislike, traits which people might trust or distrust. In spite of any dislike or mistrust people continue to deal with each other. What really counts, in a relationship, is respect. Respect which includes consideration of the other person's agenda and personal dignity. In reality respect for an individual is achieved with insights into their strengths and limitations. Sometimes, however, people employ a false display of character to mislead others in general, maybe to project a better personal image, maybe even to mask their selfish agenda. In any case they would lead the other parties astray by simply telling a lie – a mere act of deception. Once discerned, however, this may unravel the relationship. So common are such deceptive ploys that most people use caution in dealing with others. Through experience many take the position that others must earn their respect, through honesty in words and sincerity in actions. Out of such an earned relationship may come friendship. With respect embodied in every encounter the resulting bond is unfettered friendship. Such friendship entails that one tolerates any differing opinion of others regardless of ethnic traits or personal creed.

Life has its emotional moments sometimes filled with a feeling of grandeur, sometimes steeped in gloom. The positive moments usually instill a sense of well-being, full of roses and splendour. Alas, roses also possess prickly thorns. So does life. Life has its stressful moments, episodes of failures, sequences going from bad to worse. In such stressful situations it is tough to decide what's best to do. Worse yet, stressful situations usually demand a decision in a hurry. So decisions likely are made in a blur, a blur tinted with any emotional baggage of the moment. The challenge, in such circumstances, is to keep one's sanity, to try and think straight and to do so above the troublesome strife. The urge is to seek solace in a cozy haven - some place peaceful and quiet. Alas, if found, it brings only a momentary relief, a respite from the fray, because the stressful situation likely remains unresolved. If resolved by others then the outcome probably is against one's interest. More often than not one has an inkling of a stressful situation in the making. The tendency, however, is to ignore this blip on one's personal radar, probably hoping the situation would not come to pass. One ought to heed such early warning signals, to then give some thought to the situation, about how they would be personally affected, about what they could possibly do as events unfold. By doing so they are allowing their mind, not their emotions, to decide what to do and when to do it. The outcome may well be out of their control but, at least, they made a conscious effort to be involved. Nothing ventured, nothing gained. The challenge is to accept that whatever one does, whether deliberately or impulsively, may have consequences others might not tolerate. As long as one's actions were done with a conscious effort to be fair then let the chips fall where they might. Life's not perfect and likewise so will your actions.

Wanting one's way is a natural desire, such as in each day-to-day activity and routine. Egged on by such a desire many would, without a moment's hesitation, use circumstances, even people, to their advantage, cajoling others, as the need may be, to do their bidding. But such cajoling can be trying and even fruitless. For others have their own ideas and priorities. What might happen is that one may end up doing most of what needs to be done. Still, there are times when one has no choice but to rely on others. In that respect what's in it for them ? Furthermore, sometimes pursuing a dream blindly is asking for trouble. So there may come a time when one has to decide whether or not to pursue what was started. Once the dream is completed, or abandoned, it is time to move on. That's how life is lived to the full, namely, with a personal tolerance for all outcomes and actions of others particularly those adverse. And then, more importantly, move on afresh with no emotional regrets.

# Being Humane

Changing for the better will take effort as well as a possible change in one's mind-set. Tolerance, for sure, ought to be an integral part of this. To be tolerant, however, may not come easy. Usually one has to override the natural tendencies of the emotional sways in particular the seven deadly sins. It helps, therefore, to understand how to counteract these instinctive tendencies. This is the focus of the section. Hopefully such understanding will let the reader be compassionate in their actions. By acting in a humane and merciful manner we give of ourselves to others and, in the process, we secure a source of endless joy by the goodwill within. I suggest that you pursue, after reading a paragraph or so, an in-depth reflective moment on the topic.

## A COMMON DILEMMA

*symbiosis of mind and body*
*between extremes*
*the emotional factor*

Keeping the mind and the body together is a natural preoccupation - such as the body signalling, through hunger pangs, the need for nourishment and the mind consciously goes about getting food and drink, or as the mind senses imminent danger and the body, impulsively, scampers away. But sometimes turmoil comes between the two. Turmoil which hardly is given a second thought; such as the mind demanding, at times, that the body performs beyond the usual endurance thresholds into regions of stressful pain, a body which usually concerns itself with creature comfort and metabolism of the functions underneath the epidermal surface, a body which, periodically, seeks energy by means of nourishment and replenishment through restful slumber. But the bodily functions are often subservient to an inner drive betwixt the ears and within the cranium. It is, namely, the whims and fancies of the mind, a mind which sometimes seeks power way beyond the epidermal surfaces, a mind that might wander off to the outer reaches of the heavenly galaxies, a mind that might want to probe and comprehend the inner workings of molecules, a mind that may vigorously push the body to seek, such as in the heat of passion, the pleasure domes of exciting sensations and symphonic sound. This apparent crossed purpose in objectives often challenges the symbiosis between the mind and the body.

To be consciously aware of what's on the left and to the right is an instinctive prerogative. A prerogative which lends itself to other complimentary opposites: such as up and down, to and fro, black and white, yes and no. Such binary sets are akin to yin and yang, body and soul, good and evil. As for good and evil it is, for many, mostly between touching evil and bestowing loving kindness. This concept could be depicted as a guardian angel sitting on the right, exhorting goodness, while a provoking devil hovers atop the left. The choice seems to be between the boring blahs of goodness and the adrenaline rush of impish behaviour. The action taken is likely somewhere between saintly charity and self-centered gain. Sometimes the action taken is a conscious effort. Sometimes it is subliminal. Occasionally, though, an individual would mask, or at least try to mask, their ulterior motive in their agenda. Whenever that is attempted they ought to contemplate that their friends and acquaintances just might pretend to go along with the charade. At the same time these folks likely suspect, perfectly well, the ulterior motive. Needless to say, almost everyone could be accused of such a ploy at one time or another. To understand such logic and thinking you ought to reflect, now and then, on your own self-centered ways and habits. Hopefully, this is to gain an insight on the give and take, if any, you do while dealing with others. For instance, whether your tendency is to win, regardless of how, or to give in with little resistance. By doing so you now perceive how others view the mettle of your character.

For most people their ordinary day follows a familiar pattern. It is a personal protocol that is predictable and often taken for granted. It follows a pattern that likely evolved from past trials and errors. In other words, it was arrived at through personal experience. At times they may be tempted to do what they really desire but then hesitate once possible consequences dawned on them. Still many times their focus is on what, to them, is the right thing to do and what they deem to be in their own best interest. The resulting action taken sometimes is seen, to an outside observer, to be questionable. This might be truly so, for people do things for the strangest reasons. Sometimes it is done on the spur of the moment. Many times action is taken without knowing all the facts. Likewise many times the action taken seems to be out of kilter, unusual and without any apparent justification, even out of character. In other words, people are, at times, unpredictable. Their decisions seem occasionally to be emotionally driven rather than logical thinking. Gaining insights into the emotions might help one to understand such scenarios. More importantly, such understanding may lead one to realize the cause for one's own peculiar habits and unique personal ways. Such understanding, however, is difficult to gain, for it takes time and effort to analyse and accept. But it is a quest that is worthwhile pursuing should you desire peace of mind and equanimity in your life.

## THE THINGS PEOPLE DO

> *listen to the heart*
> *emotional behaviour*
> *opportunities are fleeting*

As life unfolds there are moments which are uplifting. There are also intervals of joy. There are likewise times of positive outcomes. Such moments lend themselves to a personal sense of well being. But, alas, there are also adverse times. There can be periods of disappointing setbacks. There might even be an occasional feeling of emptiness. But such is life. It is much like a bed of roses with petals of beauty but also prickly thorns. Such moments bring, for most if not all, an emotional slant to one's outlook. Happy times tend to make you light-hearted and carefree. Painful situations tend to cause apprehension and fear, a dread of what is to come. Believing that it will only get worse is natural. This dread, in turn, tends to blank out any logical thinking. The result is, for many, difficulty deciding what to do. A decision would likely be made in a daze. In such circumstances it is common for another party to suggest what to do. Such a suggestion may seem to be appropriate and applicable. But often what is suggested could benefit the other party more. It is at such times that you might be better off to rely on your gut feeling. So one must trust the instinctive impulse that comes from within. In that respect the decision taken ought to come from the heart. For sure, such a decision takes into account your self interest. So whenever you are confronted with a difficult choice of action, listen to your heart.

It is common for people to act just on an impulse: maybe they want to seize an opportunity before it passes, maybe it was due to an emotional reaction to the moment. Often impulsive behaviour happens without regard, or thought, as to possible unpleasant consequences, such as a detrimental setback. Such is the potential consequence for any action done in anger. Once anger is shown then the angry outburst is what is often remembered about the event. What took place before the angry outburst, however, is likely a different story. Many times the angry antagonist acted, beforehand, in a calm and collective manner. Who knows, they might have even counted to ten, slowly, before their outburst. But somehow the provoking situation prevails. And then the outburst happens. With the angry action there may be a momentary feeling of satisfaction. But the long-term aftermath usually entails a personal sense of guilt for overstepping the bounds of social decorum. A possible consequence of the episode is the loss of mutual trust that once existed. This fallout could be irreparable should the other party honestly believe that they did not contribute, in any way, to the cause of the outburst. Likely there are many factors and explanations, but not all of them might be discerned by both parties; maybe some are justifiable, maybe not. Such is the quandary of a quarrel. Most times the situation, alas, will not be resolved in an amicable way. Thus closure may never come to pass. Accepting such a difference is tough. But that is reality. What people often do is to let the open wound fester and sour; likely they want the other party to make amends. But that possibility hardly is going to happen. For that to happen it might need a change in personal traits and character. That aspect is what each party, especially the antagonist, has to consider for the situation to be resolved. That reality has to be acknowledged before closure happens.

Each new morning brings with it something to do, new challenges and issues to be resolved: sometimes complex, like finding a job; sometimes simple, such as what to wear. These issues usually set the tone for the day. At the same time each issue will have an outcome which depends on what one does. In turn, each outcome will depend on circumstances prevailing at the time action is taken. Each decision, including that of doing nothing, has its own sequences and consequences: sequences such as what others do in response to one's action, consequences which ascertain what it is possible to do next. Often the sequences and consequences are not discerned until one takes action.

Many times people wish, after the fact, that they knew then what they know now. But sometimes a decision must be made in a hurry. It might be a matter of seizing the opportunity of the moment, of making use of a situation which may never happen again. Such are the challenges in making a decision. In that respect how events unfold is a unique experience and quite often different from one person to the next. Sometimes one gets lucky. Sometimes one loses out. But often people reflect on what could have been whenever they dwell on the many possible outcomes, even if they should actually gain. Should events turn out to be rewarding, one after another, then such success tends to bolster personal self worth and confidence. Alas, success also tends to breed arrogance. On the other hand, failure after failure tends to lower self esteem and even diminish one's verve. Such bad experience can be humbling. But whether one wins or loses one ought to keep in mind that luck can change. So if you are lucky then you ought to be modest and thankful. But if you encounter setback after setback then you ought to consider what could have caused the situation and take appropriate action; such as how to gain the co-operation of others, how to judge circumstances, and, most of all, how not to tempt fate. More importantly, no matter what happens one should attempt to gain understanding with each experience as well as to accept whatever fate befalls one with humility and hope.

## A BALANCED PERSPECTIVE

*mind over matter*
*tit for tat*
*the power of the mind*
*having the heart, the mind and the will*

From time memorial quite a few have given thoughtful consideration to the contrasting nature of the bodily wants and the soulful quest for truths: the yin and yang of our being, the good and evil in all, the struggle between the bodily sensual desires and the ethical wishes of the mind, the intertwine of the physical urges and the spiritual yearnings. Also contemplated is how the bodily wants are so demanding for instant gratification while the mind ponders, periodically, upon what matters for meaningful existence. Likewise contemplated is how readily many succumb to sensual impulses without much thought seemingly given to the whys and wherefores, as well as for concern of others, until after the fact. Many would like to discern why. To do so is not an easy task, for, by and large, the desires of a passionate body tend to overwhelm the reasoning of the mind. By and large, the wishes of the body are self-centered and often at the expense of others. To temper these urges you might need to know more about the emotional pulls as well as an understanding of the traits commonly called the deadly sins. Through such knowledge one might be able to consider the emotional sways before taking action. It could be a case of mind over matter.

Intimate relationships are rarely cut and dry. Any related interactions tend to have a certain amount of give and take. Sometimes one gains, other times the alter ego benefits. There is, of course, also a sense of fair play and tit for tat. And that's how flexible such relationships are. Beyond such a relationship, however, people tend to be exact. Each exchange and interaction tends to have a degree of finality. Any give, or take, depends on circumstances. For instance, nothing would be expected should charity be extended to a total stranger, although some hope that the favour will be returned one future day by someone else. At times, however, such an appeal for help may be far from genuine. It might be merely a guise for gaining your attention for a sympathetic ear or perhaps a deceptive ploy. There is usually a crestfallen feeling once such a deception is discerned. After a couple of such encounters many tend to ignore appeals from others, especially strangers. But what if such an appeal is for real ? It would be so unkind if one could help but didn't. At least one ought to discern how genuine is the plea. Whatever help given is better than nothing at all, hopefully it is more than just a kind word. Such an act of kindness flows from the heart, a deed which tends to bring an inner joy, a joy that brings a calm which is positive for the soul, a calm which seems to soothe any tension within. Such an inner joy comes about only through an act of loving kindness.

Everyone needs psychological space - sufficient room for cognitive growth and personal contemplation, not every waking minute but a quiescent moment to muse and ponder. Once such a psychological moment is gained one is at ease and willing to face the challenges of the day. The beauty of such a moment is the mental calm it brings. Alas, that calm can be disrupted by an intrusive incident, such as an unexpected disturbance or the aggressive action of another. The natural reaction, of course, is to be upset. The instinctive reaction is to deal harshly with the moment and any opponent. In reacting with venom, however, keep in mind that any bit of violence tends to breed more violence. It would therefore be more constructive not to give in to any emotional rage, otherwise this might escalate out of control into an emotional incident. Sometimes being upset can be contained, but not always. To ensure containment of the instinctive emotional response one must be mentally prepared long before such upsetting incidents materialize. It won't be easy, because from early infancy one succumbs easily to the natural sways of the emotions. Now one has to change one's usual mind-set and not to give in to the emotions, especially the impulses of the seven deadly sins. Thus, for instance, one must now avoid sarcasm and criticism. To achieve such a mind-set one needs to be compassionate and humane. This, of course, entails that others are treated the same way as one would like and expect to be treated. Hopefully, that will be reciprocated.

It's difficult to exclude the emotions from whatever action people take. From early infancy the emotions have been an integral part of their being. So integral are the emotions to their make-up that, even in maturity, they, now and then, would let the emotions sway their action over any reasoning of the mind. That's the challenge one faces should one wish to give up any irritating habits and to overcome any irksome quirks. Still, it is possible to do so, even for hard-liners it is do-able. For there are many instances whereby fate and circumstances have coerced individuals, even hard-liners, to eventually change. What it takes is a personal willingness. As the saying goes - where there is a will, there's a way. What this involves are three natural attributes: a certain mind-set, the action of will power and the zealous urging of the heart. The mind provides the conscious thought. The will is the forceful zeal. The heart assures sincerity and hope. As a matter of fact very often, in ordinary life, these qualities must be synergized to achieve personal success. A common cause of failure, for example, is a lack of personal conviction and confidence. It seems that no trust is placed in the urging of the heart. To change within one must look beyond an agenda of self interest and personal comfort. One ought to focus instead on the positive, such as a caring disposition. To change within entails the combined effort of the heart and the mind with the energy, for synergy, coming from the will. In other words, should one desire any change in one's ways then one must have the heart, the mind and the will.

## CONFRONTING ANGER

*two wrongs don't make a right*
*defending one's interest*
*fighting in a passive way*
*going beyond one's point of view*

What can be disturbing to stumble upon is an angry dispute in progress, people in rage. It can be frightful. That's the scary situation one may create upon becoming angry. Sad to say, an angry situation may come about for no apparent reason. Here is such a story. A few years ago I got momentarily angry while driving. There was another driver bobbing and weaving through traffic, he then slipped in front of me. Well, I became angry. So, in turn, I accelerated past and, impulsively, cut in front of him. Now there were two driving maniacs on the road. My action failed to consider the potential danger to myself, other drivers and anyone else who might get in the way. In retrospect, fighting fire with fire very often is silly, for it commonly leads to a no-win situation. Worse yet, there are individuals who would instigate a confrontation on purpose, because they enjoy provoking others. But not everyone drawn into a dispute can cope with the subsequent confrontation. Besides, two angry wrongs hardly make the situation right. As to my traffic story, the other driver once again got in front of me. It seems that he wanted me to stop and continue the discussion physically. But I eluded him and so we went our separate ways. Now I let angry drivers pass me by, left and right. Now in angry moments I count to ten before uttering a word, or reacting in any way. Now, after counting to ten, I pursue a pacifist approach. One such approach, a common action of the colonial past, is to kill the other party with kindness. It has been, and probably still is, effective.

In the wild, a hostile confrontation is common within the animal kingdom. In such encounters the norm is to fight or take flight, to run away and, perhaps, fight another day. Standing one's ground and fighting takes courage. It also takes the flow of adrenaline to ready the body for combat. Adrenaline flows readily with the least ripple of anger. Most times all it takes is a bellicose behaviour, like the roar of a lion, growling and shouting to get the body all pumped up. Growling and shouting may also, hopefully, frighten off the opponent. That was once the situation people faced, and instinctively reacted to, in the primal epoch. Thus anger is a natural survival instinct which prepares your body for battle, to fight, to defend personal possessions, to protect a self-centered agenda, to thus get your own way. In today's world, however, one has to co-exist with others, to share at times, as well as to respect the rights of others. To achieve peaceful co-existence one may need to curb any natural anger. That involves a change in one's natural behaviour and instinctive reaction. That will take a lot of self-discipline and, more importantly, a change in one's usual attitude and mind-set.
-

Most times people talk and interact cordially and peacefully. They express personalized viewpoints and opinions in words, phrases and gestures, sometimes with a touch of emotion. This is the usual exchange between people - until there is a difference in opinion. Sometimes this is easily resolved, sometimes not. Should there be stubborn differences then the combative instinct may click in. Then the adrenaline starts to flow. Combat commences with the weapon readily at hand. Words. Differing viewpoints may be accentuated shrilly and angrily, even with vile insults. The exchange may then become physical, maybe starting with gestures then perhaps blows. Any sense of civility seems to have vaporized, being replaced with primal rage. Any thoughts of logic and fair play now are abandoned, especially of caging the rage. Common sense dictates that one ought to walk away, for hardly anything constructive now could be reached. The best that the parties involved could do is to agree to disagree. Thus not saying another word might be the most appropriate action to take. Who knows, maybe both parties have a valid viewpoint, not unlike a coin with a face on both sides. Only time will tell. In the meantime shut up, even if you are right.

To overcome anger one needs to know why people become angry. Anger plagues people of all ages: children have temper tantrums should events unfold not to their liking, the same can be said of grown-ups young and old. Anger is their way of expressing that they want to have their own way. Anger stems from an instinctive reaction to an unpleasant situation. Anger is a trait to protect one's well being as well as any selfish interests. The difficulty is that someone angry will not be reasonable and fair. All you can do is to let an angry person know that you understand where she/he is coming from and acknowledge such viewpoint. But that is only one side of the equation. How the angry party reacts is the other side of the equation and beyond your control. All you can do is to respect whatever they decide to do, right or wrong, and state your position on the matter without any emotion shown. By acting outwardly cold-heartedly, you might be able to control your own personal anger. Whatever they decide to do next is their choice, now it's up to you to take it or leave it, win or lose. In other words, total acceptance of any outcome is your way to show understanding. As to acquiring understanding, well, that takes patience. No one can teach you that, you must be willing to wait and learn.

## HAVING NO RESPECT

*winning*
*getting their own way*
*being disdainful*
*accepting others as they are*

Winning is what counts to many whenever they deal with others. To win seems to reinforce their self-importance, of being in charge and control. Alas, winning is fleeting, a momentary event, for not too often, if ever, does winning go on and on. Yet there are individuals who, as a result of winning consistently, are under the delusion that they are going to win all the time. What they fail to see is the fallacy, namely, that the law of averages, as someone else so nicely puts it, is going to clobber them. [Unless they cheat, but then is that really winning ?]. At the same time it needs to be mentioned that there is nothing wrong with winning. For many it represents a lot of personal sweat and tears. The resulting win is an exhilarating feeling and boosts morale. What matters is how the win was gained. To win by whatsoever means, such as by hook or by crook, is a covetous act not worth the resulting gloat. A true winner gains respect but a contrived winner gains loathing. Very likely the contrived mind got started with an envious thought of success. Sometimes winners overlook, perhaps not wanting to remember, that they were once just a face in the crowd, and who had a lot to learn. With time and effort they reached that moment of winning glory. Now they may feel to be above it all. What they ought to remember is that a person is never too old to learn, including winners. Because you never stop learning from mistakes and failures no matter how much you know and can do. Each breaking day brings something new to learn. Keep in mind also that it is through learning the mind, and the person within, grows.

Getting their own way is what many spiteful individuals strive to do. To make matters worse, they usually don't care about anyone else's agenda but their own. So concern for others commonly is given very little, if any, consideration. Often they would use whatever worldly guile, or subterfuge, openly or craftily, so as to get others to do their bidding. Wanting their fantasy to be a reality is their aim. Should they become aware of their actions impacting others it is usually after the fact. This likely leads to a public relations act. If so, they then become contrite, perhaps showing an 'if I *had known'* despair. Upon seeing such expressed contrition many affected individuals might deem the intrusive act to be an oversight. But, alas, that is not to be, for the perpetrator does not perceive the forgiving reaction as a precaution to be careful and considerate next time. Rather, the forgiving action is interpreted to be a sign of weakness and thus the other party will not be, in the future, a stumbling block. Co-operating with such individuals can be challenging, for they will not change until they encounter failure after failure. The sum total of any action they take is that someone is going to get hurt, whether themselves or others. Pity. It is understandable, therefore, for individuals who believe they are going to be used, in this manner, to take steps to protect their interests dealing with such people. Whatever happens is likely a tragedy in the making. Finally, here is a thought to keep in mind: those who sneakingly want to get their own way usually are green with envy.

Some people who have a great job think less of those with a lesser job, even less of those who are weak and downtrodden, like the poor. This attitude is common in the business world, where the elite have power and prestige, money to burn too. They go about their business brimming with confidence. They behave as if the prosperity of the global village depends on their know-how and talent, as if the economic framework, without them, would collapse into chaos. No doubt they think highly of themselves. Often they, in a genteel way, would request others, especially their staff, to do their bidding. Naturally, those imposed upon would appear willing and able, politely requesting clarification if need be. The job then gets done. Needless to say, any request they make tantamount to a demand. In their myopic vision they perceive the condescending behaviour of others to be awe and admiration, even respect. What many of them fail to see is the fear others have of their wrath. So those imposed upon try not to get in their way and not to upset them. If that ever happens they could become vindictive, sometimes clandestinely, sometimes boldly and openly. How dare this low life refuse to do their bidding. This is the customary style of many high and mighty people towards those deemed to be of no importance. To outsiders this summarizes the many opinions which they have of people in power. But what was now just described is the attitude of people who are jealous and envious of those in positions of power. For most competent people in positions of power are not jealous or envious of others, rather they admire, if nothing else, those with abilities and talents greater than theirs. Furthermore, people in power tend to respect their subordinates since they value the assistance and help the subordinates provide. True, at times they seem to make heartless and ruthless decisions. But whenever they do so it is usually a corporate or organizational call based on a constructive objective rather than a vindictive choice. In other words, the decision is made without any hard feelings, a decision which hardly anyone envies making.

What is valued by everyone is self-esteem and dignity. Thus they expect others to show respect. In this regard respect is a common courtesy shown at the start of a relationship and thus taken for granted. In spite of this there are some people who demand respect, likely because they believe themselves to be of importance. What they need to realize, however, is that respect is a natural reciprocal gesture willingly shown in any human interaction. Respect is thus mutually taken for granted at the start of a relationship. Respect entails accepting others for what they are, as they are, warts and all, including funny ways and habits, for no one is perfect. Respect takes into consideration that each has limitations and faults, opinions too, opinions which could differ from one's own. So by demanding respect you are asking for mere lip service, for respect transcends mere words and kind gestures. Respect comes from the heart.

## CURBING THE APPETITES

*satisfying the inner urges*
*gaining inner control*
*a contemplative moment*

Every morning people awake to then follow, more or less, a set routine for the day. A routine so familiar, to them, that many lapse, at times, into a zombie-like pattern of activities, sometimes seemingly indifferent to any human flurries that may happen around them. The urge, occasionally, is to shake off such monotony, an itch to do something new and exciting. So they proceed to do whatever that takes, such as surrounding themselves with creature comfort paraphernalia. Name it, they got it. Often, however, boredom creeps into their thoughts once the novelty wears off, a boredom bordering on a void echoing within their being. To alleviate this feeling many seek excitement in entertaining pursuits, possibly causing wanton behaviour. Such pleasurable distractions seem to help obliterate the void. But, somehow, the emptiness creeps back into their mind with the next lull in their life. Most then venture forth again to seek excitement. And so the cycle continues ad nauseam. In contrast there are many who decide to sit down and listen to the echoing void within. Most times it leads to wondering about the hereafter, about what is the end all and be all to their existence. So they pursue their quest commonly in cyberspace, libraries and talks. Some study about the rituals of past and present civilizations, their myths and their gods, about religions and beliefs in the life hereafter. Those who pursue this path may take it one step further, making soul searching contemplation, perhaps joining a religious group, practising self control of their inner passions, seeking inner calm. To get inner peace, however, one needs to discipline the emotions. One has to put a clamp onto the sensuous impulses, as much as humanly possible. Quite a few have spent their entire life trying to acquire such self-control. A few go as far away as possible from society into a monastic way of life. For those in the secular world, however, achieving such self-control is not an easy task. It involves, for instance, a conscious effort to monitor the consequences of one's actions and to muzzle the habitual ways of the emotions. That's a tall order. Still, it can be done: all it takes is a focused mind, a zealous heart and a determined will.

One cannot do without eating and sleeping. After all, the body needs nourishment and rest to survive. The daily partaking of food and liquid can be a tasty and enjoyable experience, in fact some do so to excess. Such is the instinctive vice of gluttony. As for those of average weight, they likely believe that they don't have an obsession with food. What they likely have difficulty with is maybe one of the other instinctive vices: a seething flash of rage, covetous glances, lustful yearnings, haughty pride, greedy hands or *can wait 'til tomorrow'* syndrome of laziness. Well, that is not the case of people leaving the general population and venturing, voluntarily, into a cloistered and austere monastic retreat for a short duration. After being cloistered, for a while, the instinctive vice which commonly invades their thoughts is the craving for food. No wonder it is said that the way to a man's heart is through his stomach. That's why people wine and dine those whose hearts and minds they want to inveigle. Such is the passion nestling within each one's stomach. What it takes to overcome this passion is, of course, self-control. This is what anyone overweight should practise, namely eat less in a gradual way. To augment this endeavour they may have to drown the subsequent hunger pangs with liberal libations of water. As for the reader, you ought to leave the dinner table slightly hungry. You will find that within twenty minutes any pangs of hunger dissipate. Incidentally, for those who dwell within a cloistered community, they control this passion by means of periodical fasting now and then. As a matter of fact, to have control over your passions begins by first regulating your food intake. Afterwards you can better tackle any habitual vice. Of course, at the start there will be doubts. Keep in mind this is just the start of the quest; inner peace comes much later, yes, much much later.

Inner peace requires one to go beyond the mental struggle with more than emotional vices. Inner peace also requires one, believe it or not, to be compassionate and humane.

Now and then as people go about their personal business there will be moments of contemplative calm, times when the heart and the mind are in synch. Ordinarily many utilize this reflective pause to focus on what preoccupies their minds at that moment. It might be a vexing situation. What can one do about it? Often a possible solution, through contemplation, springs to mind. Amazingly, however, a few waste the moment to just mope and worry, to dwell on what could possibly go wrong. No thought at all would be given to resolving the situation. On the other hand, quite a few take the time, if there is no pressing personal issue, to reflect on what life is all about, about the whys and wherefores to life. But such musing quickly vaporizes once they wade back into engulfing personal routines and activities. Incidentally, such peaceful pauses are ideal to clear the mind of any clutter. It is also ideal for constructive planning: things to do, places to go or people to see. By being constructive you rid the mind of worrisome issues and thus taste a bit of tranquillity and inner calm. But often such constructive thoughts are displaced quickly by the personal demons within, demons demanding your passionate attention: perhaps gluttonous cravings, vengeful rage, envious desires, lustful wishes, self-centered pride, voracious greed, or slothful behaviour. Such demons can become so disturbing that there could be uncorked a sense of frustration and despair. Naturally, the challenge is to put the contemplative moments to constructive use by letting the demons go, let them vamoose into thin air. Here is a challenge for the heart, the mind and the will. Try it out.

## HAVE A HEART

*extending a helping hand*
*the mood of misery*
*giving from the heart*

It is natural to focus just on one's own self-interest. It is instinctive to be concerned mainly about one's welfare and the immediate family. Occasionally kindness may be extended to others as one prospers. As income escalates people accumulate luxurious possessions and treasures. In a few cases avarice becomes a never-ending story. But in the luckless world there are hordes of penniless people. Each day they are challenged as to keeping mind and body together. Finding sustenance is a daily priority which sometimes is fruitless. A sense of low esteem is reflected so vividly in their tattered attire and hygiene. It is a quandary begging for help. The divide between haves and have-nots is noticeable. What causes the divide has people speculating about it. Some are of the opinion that luck and circumstances can be the cause. Others believe many bring the situation upon themselves. Whatever the cause the fact remains that people are suffering from hunger and other wants. It is a situation each of us can help to alleviate. No matter how bad you believe your situation is, there is someone else who has it worse. Besides, you and I may find, heaven forbid, ourselves to be a have-not one day in the future. Under present circumstances are you able to help ? Whatever you give will likely make a difference. The beauty about extending a helping hand to the needy is the boost to your morale, because it is an act of love. You certainly can make a difference, a difference which likely brings a needy soul a ray of hope.

Mood is a volatile commodity which often colours one's outlook. Mood may cause some to look at a serious situation with gloom and doom while others may, in the same situation, discern humour. Mood is a highly individualistic trait which commonly puts a tint to the circumstance of the moment as well as one's emotional make-up. Mood might make one adopt an upbeat perspective or a melancholy disposition. Thus the various moods among a group of people, facing the same quandary, will impact their attitude; letting some make the best of the situation while others may mope in dismay. Mood is an emotional spectrum which permeates every layer of society: the mood of those who have it made may be miserable while those who have very little may be contented with their lot in life. The challenge one faces is not to let a temporary dismal disposition interfere with how one deals with others. For instance, a dismal disposition, if given a chance, could make one mean-spirited with a desire to spread misery. In turn the other party likely may retaliate. It could be the end of a beautiful friendship. So if you have nothing constructive to say then you ought not to say anything rather than to make a nasty remark. It is what's not said that counts. On the other hand should you be bubbling over with happiness then, by all means, spread the joy around. You might cheer the mood of others up by doing so.

Each of us has a natural propensity for wanting beautiful objects and possessing nice trinkets. For some this translates into wearing the latest fashion, maybe to frequenting trendy places, perhaps filling their homes with creature comfort gizmos. In this respect people pursue their individual passions and dreams. Most, no matter how fabulous their lifestyle may be, believe that the way they live is basic and simple. No matter how good they have it they still want more. Inevitably there will come a day when owning a new item brings not joy but an emotional let down. The state of mind the new possession begets is boredom, perhaps boredom with a miserable disposition. Let's face it, when this happens then the message is that what you now own, and have, is more than necessary to satisfy your basic needs. After all, there is only so much a person can eat, wear and use to keep her/him in creature comfort. What it also means is that it is time to change a personal perspective beyond personal welfare and survival. For sure, it is not about possessing more. In a sense you are in the enviable position of being able to help others. So what's so difficult about giving of oneself? Whether that be giving of your time or money. How one decides to be charitable is a personal choice. It is just a matter of giving from the heart, a giving which would bring a ray of hope, a hope which would likely flicker out unless someone steps forward to help. Alas, many prefer not to give but to remain self-centered and thus preserve their personal state of misery, a misery without any hope. The choice is yours.

## TAKING CARE OF BUSINESS

*chasing nothing but trouble*
*a foremost thought*
*keeping it close*

For any given day not every moment awake is conducive to constructive thinking. Before that happens the mind usually first considers the status of the various tedium tasks on hand. So these are each given attention, time and energy, one to the next. Should these tasks be done with diligence and care, there is hardly any time to be bored. If anything a few might be overlooked. Most wish they could be this methodical each day. But this is hardly the case. Just the thought of the tedium ahead tends to numb the mind. In many instances a task which is done gets a courtesy glance of review before being hurriedly completed. Sometimes a task is not given any attention until timing is critical. In the beginning it was probably not like that, particularly at work. In those earlier days there were likely fire and fury within, an eagerness to do a thorough job. With the passage of time, however, such attentiveness may be dimmed probably through repetition and boredom. The zeal may have vaporized. There is now a hesitation and tardiness to do any work. Soon there is probably a lack of commitment, an urge to get away from the humdrum, to do something out of the ordinary, maybe something just for the excitement.

The temptation is to give into this urge. For those who follow such temptation, the outstanding tasks go by the wayside as they pursue amusement and fun. Pursuing such fantasy may tickle their senses, apparently giving them new life. Now what they may overlook is the security of job and home, as if both will be there no matter what they pursue and do otherwise. That's how tardiness can affect one's way of life.

There are times when one feels no urge to do a stitch of work, no desire to put out an ounce of effort. Of course the furthest thought is to be lethargic and slothful. Surely lethargy and laziness, in this regard, are the traits of somebody who lets everyone else hustle without lifting a finger, except perhaps to offer words of platitudes or maybe to criticize what's being done. Often whatever is said tends to upset the people working. How could anyone just look on while work goes begging ? How did they get to be so lazy ? It's difficult to say, even for them. Such a state of mind likely developed gradually in stages. They seem to start by being insensitive about the feelings of others. In the process they overlooked any common courtesy, like pronouncing names every which way, except the way the namesake wants. In essence lethargy seems to narrow a person's focus into a beam of thought solely upon a self-centered agenda. In turn they want personal causes to be enhanced by, and through, the time and effort of others. Lethargy is a common symptom of someone who, often unintended, cares not for others or, worse yet, has no problem doing so. And so such individuals have no desire to hear, much less to know, what others have to say. What they seem to disregard is consideration and respect for others. But without these qualities it is difficult to foster a trusting relationship. Now and then you ought to mentally step back and think about how you deal with others, such as whether you keep your word and promise or show consideration in whatever you do. The conclusion you reach ought to correlate with the degree of trust, or lack of, others have in you.

In whatever endeavour a person pursues there is an initial hope for the best and for at least some success. Once the project is under way there is gained a better idea of what it is going to take for the job to be done, especially any reliance on others to do specific tasks or to make relevant decisions. Needless to say, such dependency requires the work to be done in a timely fashion. Unfortunately this is not always achieved. It's worse if these others are in control such as one's elder or one's boss. Often one continues working in anticipation of their co-operation. The sad aspect to this wait is the extra pressure of stress and frustration. Care ought to be taken to show no anger, otherwise such an outburst could cause further delay. Care also ought to be taken to be cordial. What ought to have been done, from the start, is to have an idea what makes such individuals tick, to speak in a vernacular language they understand. Needless to say, you ought to be firm on what is rightfully yours even while giving and taking in any exchange. Whatever is done remember to **keep your friends close but keep your enemies closer**. This way you can be more realistic in your expectations.

## SWAYS OF THE HEART

*the emotional factor*
*for better or for worse*
*compassion*

Within each human heart flows an emotional pulse which can be difficult, at times, for others to read. One minute there might be a welcome smile but the next moment an icy stare. So many factors can activate the pulse and control the moment, such as either a stressful situation not apparent, debilitating health, a setback, or perchance the weather. Also common are impulsive behaviours seemingly without rhyme or reason, to do what you feel like at that moment. In general, though, a person tends to be logical in behaviour. Any interaction with others usually starts with a pleasantry which may then evolve into a give and take discussion. Instinctively many want to take control of the topic until interest is shown by those listening. Such exchanges happen daily everywhere. How the controlling party steers the conversation is discretionary. Sometimes the controller steers a neutral course allowing a free-flowing discussion, but sometimes she/he can be cruel and mean. This is the discretion each has in any engaging talk with others. Many are the reasons why people converse: one of them is to seek friendship, a chit chat to soothe an inner tension, an audience for a troubled mind, maybe a second opinion or a reassuring word. Asking for such reassurance, however, seems to disturb some people. In that respect should you be so approached you ought to consider helping just by listening and maybe extending a hand of loving kindness. Who knows, one day you might be seeking such reassurance from someone else for **a friend in need is a friend indeed**.

As the years pass people encounter new situations and experiences. With each new encounter there usually is learnt a little bit more about human nature. In the process people become more mellow in their outlook. Still, it remains difficult to control the emotions when confronted with an upsetting situation. It is as if the emotional component has, to a certain degree, a constancy. In much the same way many believe their integral character is constant. Thus the person of yesteryear is the same one today, maybe a bit more mellow and wise. Take, for example, a personal propensity for good, a propensity which starts, of course, with being good to oneself, good also to others, usually on a selective basis, such as family, friends and acquaintances, occasionally even strangers. Such fellow individuals would be bestowed with affection and care. As the years pass such love and affection more than likely increase. It could be said that, in more ways than one, there is a personal change for the better. But this is just one side of the equation, for there could be a nasty streak, a meanness which might, at times, chill the blood of those being the target, a streak which likely started in a somewhat innocent manner, such as an impish gesture, the butt of a joke. Over time, however, this habit tends to escalate to devilish enjoyment, definitely a change for the worse as far as some individuals are concerned. In this respect the overall personal emotional streak of each person also changes with the passage of time, either for the better or for the worse, rarely does it stay constant. You ought to give a thought as to the present status of your emotional streak, namely, has it improved for the better or is there degradation for the worse ?

There is no doubt who is the first love of your life: it is, of course, yourself. It is a love which gives you a reason for living, a purpose to care. But sometimes this love can be so self-centered that you will forego the interests of others, perhaps inadvertently, often intrusively. Such is the zeal of this self ardour. Such can be the intensity of this devotion. How this shows in someone's actions can be disturbing, much like the temper tantrum of a child who wants her/his way, or the violating action of a male with rapacious intent. What these actions portray is a lust for power, a will to control, by hook or by crook. Most times people will not stop such zealous pursuits until they are humbled with the ugly face of failure. Alternatively, they may cease once they become ashamed of the misery and grief they wrought on others. How to cool such ardour in one's ordinary pursuits ? It is not as difficult as might be imagined. What it takes is a certain frame of mind, a frame of mind with benevolence as well as a willing attitude coupled with loving kindness. To achieve such a frame of mind you need not change much in the way of your routines and habits. That's the beauty of it. The tough part is to be consciously reasonable and considerate as well as to forego any shortfall of others with no vengeful feeling. Concurrently, any praise and credit you gain is to be accepted with humility. In time a sense of contentment and well-being is enjoyed. But some people are uncomfortable about being always considerate, about not dishing out misery and gloom to people they dislike. Likewise, it may be difficult to walk away from a quarrel without the urge to throttle the opponent. Such malicious thinking ought to be put aside, for ill-will begets ill-will. Of course, if one is attacked then, by all means, retaliate. If the other party gets hurt, well, so be it. So no matter how upsetting a situation may become always be willing to extend a sympathetic ear, particularly to mean-spirited individuals. Believe it or not, such sympathy shows compassion and pity, a compassion which comes from a loving heart.

## ADMITTING ONE'S MISTAKES

*telling it as it is*
*showing consideration*
*mindful of playing games*

Everyone is special, special since each person is unique, unique because every individual has a distinct mix in her/his character of talent, traits and experience no one else has. So each one pursues a personal path with this unique character mix. Sometimes, in the process, good fortune falls one's way. Some seem to be of the opinion that they are the sole architect of this, but fate also plays a part. During prosperous times quite a few would lull themselves into complacency, taking their good fortune for granted. But the law of averages eventually catches up. When that happens the smile fades from their face. Should setback follows setback the outlook may become grim, self-confidence may wane, errors tend to creep into whatever they do. Still, many are able to wade past this phase of ill-luck. Quite a few, however, would mire themselves in misery. Sometimes, in this melancholy disposition, they might ascribe a setback as a deliberate act. Any genuine apology would not be accepted even though it might be an honest mistake. It is also common to blame others for causing the ill-fortune but, whether so or not, this is not going to resolve matters. Besides the situation warrants constructive thinking, such as taking an objective look at how these setbacks came about, for what may seem proper then to do may have been far from appropriate. Nothing should now be taken for granted, possible alternatives and improvements ought to be explored. Of course, in the process, a mistake, by chance, could be made, so what else is new ? Mistakes have happened in the past, and will continue to do so, time and time again. If you are afraid of making a mistake and then give in to this fear there is little hope of learning, much less personal growth. Making mistakes is how people learn, it is a process involving trial and error, of trying again and again, of finding out what works, what doesn't, and what works better. In other words, we learn often by failing. Keep in mind that you never stop learning, no matter how learned you are.

Taking pride in one's appearance is an instinctive reflection of self esteem. Such behaviour expresses a desire for respect. But there is more to respect than apparel donned and grooming. What one says, and how it is said, also counts. Shouting and swearing, for instance, hardly helps. What certainly helps is the elegance which comes with wealth, power and prestige. But not everyone possesses these attributes. So it is a matter of showing a similar style in self confidence. What counts, especially in a long lasting relationship, are the confidence words convey and the trust personal action gains. Often such confidence and trust last a lifetime. Sometimes, however, it is lost in a flash due to a omission inadvertently made. Here is where it counts to earn up to the mistake made, the quicker the better. But often pride gets in the way about making amends. Pride banishes the thought of apologizing for the oversight shown much less the lack of consideration. Pride once again have played havoc with human nature and personal foibles in admitting to a honest mistake. To do so is commonly a humbling experience. Trust that you will admit to such errors in judgement and rectify the matter at the proper time.

People enjoy playing games. It can be the source of personal development, fun and amusement. Games come in many different forms: a contest, like in sports, a conflict resolution, such as in a video game, or hilarity as in a practical joke. Such a joke is done in fun, just in jest. But sometimes it is done with malicious intent, which could have a sordid consequence, whereby the worse is brought out in the perpetrator with the intended target likely retaliating. Occasionally both wish to win the subsequent thrust and parry, sometimes at whatever the cost, probably intent on proving personal supremacy. To now lose may be bothersome, likely a blow to an imagined feeling of invincibility. In the process arrogance could override any thought of peaceful co-existence. Stirred emotions may have gotten the upper hand. That's how pride can get the better of a person, a common mistake. In such a circumstance winning is not everything. It is how the game is played. Should the other party become highly emotional then it is very likely useless to appeal to her/his sense of reasoning. Arguing with someone who won't heed a word one may say is an exercise in futility. Until they are willing to listen to logic and reason it is a lost cause. In the interim one should take steps to get out of harm's way, to safeguard one's interests, more importantly, to remain calm with a clear and rational mind. If need be, one ought to humbly walk away. Rebutting to any taunt likely will lead to a confrontation which usually gets out of hand. In the process each may lose respect for the other. It might be the end of a cherished friendship, all due to a difference in opinion. That's how pride can get the better of you.

## BE THE ONE TO MAKE THE DIFFERENCE

*considering others*
*making an effort*
*proactive interactions*
*adjusting with the times*

Not everyone on this planet has a structured and stable way of life. It is, for those unfortunates, a daily struggle, their constant focus is to feed a nagging hunger, clothing and shelter usually are of secondary concern. Fate has not been kind, at times their next meal is one of hope. Resigned to their fate they await, with hardly any qualms, whatever hardship comes their way. Even then they somehow readily burst into laughter at the tender touch of humour. In contrast to such an easygoing disposition is the uptight behaviour of some whose bread, in common parlance, is well buttered. Their concern seems to drift into mesmerized thoughts on what next to acquire, not out of necessity but out of desire. In like manner they guardingly shield the many advantages they enjoy, thus they likely would object to any civic change diminishing their social status. In spite of their bountiful plenty, misery seems part of their character, an apparent trait of meanness to those they dislike. To alleviate their misery many tend to seek comfort in pleasures and thrills, such as potent liquids and pills, perhaps psychedelic powder, so as to escape the doldrums and boredom. A few might pursue a suave savant. But, inevitably, the melancholy returns. What they likely need is a perspective other than me, me, me, an endeavour different from take, take, take. To do so entails venturing beyond their usual personal sphere, in mind and in spirit, such as an act of sincere generosity, of kindness from the heart. Besides, who is there better to help the unfortunate than those in relative security, people with confidence, people who knows how to get things done, people capable of giving without a blink ? Such individuals can be the difference to those in need, such individuals can make that difference a reality, and many do. They try to help in whatever way they can, whether individually or to a cause. In the process what they commonly experience is the joy of giving, a giving which warms the heart. As a matter of fact anyone can make the difference a reality, including you the reader of these words. All it takes is a willingness. Some may, however, find that difficult to do. Often they have a perspective centered around minding their own business. In much the same way they expect others to look out for themselves. Should they discern, in others, a motive other than a self-centered perspective it is treated with suspicion, perchance apprehensively. Thus, in general, they tend to be indifferent to what happens to others as long as they are not personally affected. But no matter how self-centered an individual can be there are moments when they feel empathy for someone in distress, sympathy for a person in need. The urge is to help. Compassion ought to be shown. A few, however, still would refrain from helping, probably not wanting to become involved. However, assistance ought to be given in whatever way possible. Every little bit counts, even though the need is greater than what any one individual could provide, for any help is better than nothing. Now is the moment to be humane and show compassion. In a retrospective reflection of your journey through life I am sure that there are moments when there was a personal hope that others would show compassion and consideration to you. Sometimes the plea fell on deaf ears, but sometimes mercy was shown. Now the table is turned and you have a chance to be merciful. Hopefully, you will extend compassion and consideration. Remember that a plea for help comes usually when least expected. Please be kind when that time comes.

Wanting to excel at anything attempted is a common desire. But such a goal involves time and effort which, for some, seems to be a luxury. As it is, they can barely cope with the immediate demands on hand. To cope they usually try to get by doing the minimum, namely, just enough to satisfy the moment. Even then many seem to go from crisis to crisis. Somehow there is attained a respite, a lull, a period of peaceful pause, time allowing recharge of body and mind. But, inevitably, the hectic times would return. Once more the tendency is to do the minimum, even though this could cause an oversight or an omission. Should this create a problem then more time and effort would be devoted to rectify the matter. Had there been due diligence the first time around this might have been avoided. In many instances the failure was caused by a lack of focus. A common retort to such comment is that they had no time for such malarkey. That might be so for their present predicament but very often one has a notion, quite early, of a problem in the making. But then nothing would be done until a crisis arises. An early ounce of prevention might have more than sufficed for the subsequent pound of cure. No doubt wanting to excel involves more than thinking and saying so, but attitude and preparation also are important. Thus the luxury of relaxing comes after the job gets done, not before. Likewise one ought to thoughtfully plan what to do and how to do it beforehand. Even with such a plan of action sometimes a person would still become discouraged and quit once any difficulty is encountered. But, who knows, this difficulty might be resolved by just a bit of perseverance or reflective assessment. That will not be known without trying. Let it be said that setbacks are common in any human endeavour. Furthermore it is through setbacks that one gains insights commonly referred to as personal experience. What it takes is resilience and mettle, not to mention a willingness to try something new. But many dread the thought of failing. On that score kindly note that many successful people would tell about their own personal failures along the journey to fortune and fame. So why should your fortune be any different ? Whether successful or not, it is trying one's best that counts. In the process knowledge and personal wisdom are gained. The beauty of success is that it usually spurs an individual to try with greater zeal. On the other hand setbacks tend to lower your confidence. Whatever the outcome with each issue faced please temper your emotional reaction by accepting success with humility and setbacks with forbearance. With such temperance the chance of success is enhanced in future challenges.

People - individuals with myriads of thoughts, desires, passions and dreams. They surround us, at times engulf us, commonly on busy thoroughfares, at boisterous meetings and social functions. Casual interactions are many. Most exchanges are brief and friendly, transactions tend to be short and simple, usually with courtesy and respect. But once in a while such a casual contact may go beyond the superficial. Occasionally friendship prospers, opinions are shared, insights are gained, a mutually beneficial relationship develops. In contrast a casual contact tends to be a bit formal, even impersonal, a protocol many adopt. One aspect to interactive skills which is unique to each person is her/his pattern of behaviour. Somehow many are able to maintain a polite decorum until they feel stressed, then the real 'me' emerges. It is this underlying behaviour which gives a sketch of the character within, such as a caring individual or, perhaps, a self-centered person. Surprisingly, some people hardly give much thought to the character so portrayed. Often close acquaintances tell them as it is. Usually positive comments are well received. But a negative remark tends to be dismissed as fluff, no matter how apt, as a result hardly any notice would be paid to a possible deviant behaviour. In that respect no one is perfect, everyone has their faults. Such faults are part of one's traits, traits which inevitably come into play with each human encounter, whether for the first time or with someone familiar. How such actions are perceived is what counts with others. Each personal action of what was said and done creates an impression. Ordinarily it wouldn't be lasting but it may impart a positive vibe or a negative barb. This may, in turn, translate into an uneventful moment or an irksome incident, or it could become momentarily memorable. So what you ought to consider is the image portrayed by your conduct, an image which, to a great extent, is within your control. In addition, whatever action you take, or decline to take, entails an outcome, favourable or not, which ought to be accepted. What might disturb any such acquiescent is an outcome contrary to expectations, such as a nasty twist not to your liking. What if things were done differently ? A thought worth speculating about, especially if you had an uneasiness and an inkling of something going wrong but took no action. Often what stops most from taking any action is time and effort which they couldn't spare, or so they say. But what makes sense is to look out for one's own interests from the start. The challenge is to do so without being a predator while warding off others. To do so you ought to keep your eyes and ears open as you go about your business, to scan the lay of the land and the people you encounter, to perceive people as individuals with unique traits and quirks, each with traits one might like and quirks one may detest. Genuine relationships, especially long-lasting ones, often involve respecting each other interests and concerns. Compromise is common. Such a proactive approach in one's dealings definitely enhances outcomes and one's well being. What might disturb some, however, is a sordid response, or a lack of reciprocity, even outright injustice. This is an issue out of your hands. This is an issue only the other party can correct. You ought to realize that such negative action is a choice which the other party decided to make. In turn, you have no choice but to accept, although perturbed, the resulting turn of events. Another one bites the dust. Just pick up the pieces and move on. At least you made an attempt to deal in good faith. Now it's time to face the next encounter.

Each generation seems to have a perspective all its own: its members have their own buzz words, tunes and rhythms they enjoy immensely, clothing and styles somewhat new, strange and, in their eyes, chic, codes of conduct hardly in writing but well-known. They seem to thrive on their episodes of glory - until the next generation takes the stage. Inevitably the next set changes the social landscape. Such pageantry is common to the human experience: a flux which comes with growth, growth which brings about constantly changing attitudes. As for the new generation, their thoughts seem to focus mostly on the evolving and shifting scene at work, at play as well as on lifestyles. But after a while they tend to seek the comfort of familiarity, a personal consistency in protocol and what takes place. A radical change to such orderliness is not appreciated. As a matter of fact no attempt to such change would be tried until deemed a necessity, even then that might be done grudgingly. What is overlooked is the static nature of such an attitude. Likewise disregarded is that as time passes there will be new ways to do things, innovative pathways which evolve from fresh ideas, new insights and scientific findings. These then trickle down into the social fabric of the general population. Thus changes come about whether an individual desires it or not. The irksome personal aspect, to many, is the transition stage involving trials and errors as well as the process of getting acquainted with the new idea and adopting to it. Coping with something new is naturally stressful, even for those desirous of change. A common way to cope is to let circumstances dictate personal change; by reacting by personal adjustment rather than thinking the process through. Hence many, likely with a hope and a prayer, would let others impose the necessary change. Letting change happen in this fashion, however, might not be in your own best interest, for people tend to act with their own self-interest foremost. So a decision made could likely benefit mostly the person making the decision. One should act in likewise fashion: that's done by taking the initiative, that involves taking control of the decision making process where possible, changing this and changing that to one's liking and benefit without affecting the overall plan. But, of course, not every change is for the better; for instance, one gets old and slides effortlessly into senility. Thus you ought to try and understand the many aspects of inevitable changes and the options you may have. Otherwise there will be moments when there is a feeling of guilt, for not doing something about a change you see coming. In contrast, taking control prepares you for what is to come, even if that be for the worse. All that you can do is to try for the best possible fit. As a result your conscience, free of guilt, may now focus on the positive, to now enjoy the fragrance of the blooming roses, to now give hope and joy to others, to perchance offer, willingly, loving kindness to everyone you meet whether familiar or new. The personal focus is all on good will, peace and love.

# *In Search of Self Control*

Being self-sufficient is a goal many of us wish to achieve. To get there entails a conscious effort to improve one's disposition, outlook and temperament. At times, however, others seem to test one's mettle and resolve. It is a learning experience. Here are some thoughts on this issue. I suggest that you pursue, after reading a paragraph or so, an in-depth reflective moment on the topic.

## CHANGING FOR THE BETTER

*making a commitment*
*having doubts*
*people and circumstances*

For one to reach above and touch the stars afar is an effort that seems next to impossible. Yet that's the kind of zeal successful people seem to have. Such zeal often is displayed inherently by those successful in sports, science and business. They want to be at the top of the heap and so they aim to be second to none. Such is the determination needed to change for the better. Alas most people are not willing to make such an effort. In fact many believe their character stays the same, year in, year out. But, in reality, nearly everyone changes in ways and personal traits as time goes by. The change could be subtle or dramatic. Likewise the change could be for the better or it might be for the worse. Only those with an intimate knowledge of a person's character can tell. A change for the worse comes easily with a self-centered agenda. But a change for the better requires one not only to be considerate but also to bridle the emotional ill-will within. To do so involves perseverance and a conscious effort.

Errors and omissions are frequent in whatever actions we take. It happens time and time again no matter how we try not to, for it is part of our nature to make mistakes perhaps by accident or through oversight. Many wish, and want, to forego any such conscious habit. So they make personal resolutions, especially at the start of a new year. Henceforth, they proclaim, in all honesty, they are going to correct the errors of their ways. Often such a resolve is sincere. Often it is so intense that there is a new psychological frame of mind. Often they follow through, at least for a short while, until a tempting situation presents itself once more. Each time this happens the resolve within might weaken little by little. The more they are tempted the greater the likelihood to succumb. Then comes **what's the use** skepticism. How to ward off such temptations is a challenge as the urge grows to lapse into former familiar ways. What ought to be considered, at the moment of resolve, is how to circumvent the moments of temptation.

Changing for the better hardly happens overnight. For such a change to be successful, one ought to ponder upon how the habit got started in the first place. This helps to ascertain the root cause or causes for the habit, which is a personal knee jerk reaction to a certain set of circumstances. So the idea is to find out what these circumstances are. In many instances a habit, such as smoking, is a personal opiate, albeit not the best, for handling a stressful situation. The next challenge is to identify who, or what, could be the cause for the habit. Many times the provocateurs are members of one's family and close acquaintances, frequently the mother-in-law or the boss. To make matters worse, these individuals do not believe that they could be the cause. So to get them to cooperate and help the change process, in any way, is likely out of the question. Besides should they be willing to do so it will definitely be on their terms and thus not to your liking. Whatever is considered for the change process it needs to be flexible. Anticipate the worse case scenario but hope for favourable circumstances. Likewise, adopt a modality to keep your cool and control your emotions no matter what. Naturally, there must be an alternate plan, commonly referred to as 'Plan B', namely, to exit quickly in case the situation becomes untenable. Finally, remember that there is only one individual on whom you can totally depend upon - namely, yourself.

## THE INFLUENCE OF OTHERS

*misery loves company*
*bias behaviour*
*as time goes by*
*the trying aspect to intimacy*

There are days when you awake with a bright outlook and a positive disposition. The day thus begins with a feeling of well-being and that life is worth living. But the mood may end once you cross paths with someone in a mean mood, someone bristling with misery. That encounter tends to tarnish your mood resulting in your attitude changing for the worse. This shows its ugliness whenever you deal with others thereafter. Often your tone now is sour. Such is the influence of a nasty temperament. The challenge, upon such a bitter encounter, is to stay positive no matter what. Try not to let any barbs upset your mood and emotions because the intention is to infect you with misery. So be on your guard and keep in mind that *misery loves company*.

Each moment awake the mind gathers information which is absorbed and simplified; data are classified and grouped, impressions are formulated into opinions. In like manner people who, from a distance, look and act alike are labeled with the same stereotyped traits. Often the label is nasty, mean and based on ethnic makeup or social status. Thus every single person within this grouping is collectively the same whether good, bad or ugly. Should your family be so libelously labeled you would be the first to object, ready to explain, in detail, how each relative is different and unique. Well, the same can be said about everyone else on this planet, namely, each has a character and personality all their own regardless of ethnic makeup or social status. Alas, such a biased label prevails in the minds of many for anyone strange and different. Worse yet, such a collective label fails to convey that every individual can change in character as they grow in knowledge and maturity. So to stereotype people with a biased label is callous and ignorant, not to mention causing irreparable harm.

Many believe that they are the architect of their own destiny as they tread upon the sands of time. Yet often it is circumstances, as encountered, which govern not only what can be done but also the chances of success. Fortunate circumstances often are taken for granted and considered proper and fitting. At the same time dismal misfortunes often are viewed as disappointingly unfair. What ought to be appreciated is any favourable circumstances and people encountered, such as the instrumental influence of those in positions of power and prestige. The company one keeps plays a part in one's self confidence. By and large they are the people who reinforces one's views and, more importantly, one's self esteem. One rarely appreciates favourable circumstances and people, however, until long after an event. Only upon reflection in later years may a thought be given to the luck encountered.

As time goes by there is a different modality in our thinking. In younger years we tend to be more open to risks but as we advance in years we tend to be more conservative.

Who knows, there may even be a change of heart. These twists and turns of life underline the need to be open to innovative ways, fresh insights and understanding. So be willing to change so that you don't mind adjusting to new circumstances.

One phase of adult life many often impulsively pursue is an intimate and close relationship. At the start there is a fervent desire to spend the rest of their earthly days together. Such a relationship could lead to living jointly together and to care for each other. Each usually takes into account the likes and dislikes of the other, of mutual giving and taking, at times mostly giving, of giving solace in moments of sorrow, of sharing joy in happy times. There is a sense of personal commitment. Soon the relationship becomes a fact of personal life and taken for granted. Still, being human, each is not perfect. So there might be an irritating habit in the other irksome enough to cause an occasional wish to be single again. But usually the moment passes with the wish forgotten. Believe it or not, there is a more difficult challenge and that is to allow quality time for the mutual partner to have an independent pursuit of her/his volition and interest. Still, hopefully, as the years pass the union grows in love and friendship. Alas, in some cases the worst happens and there is a parting of the ways. In such cases the challenge is for one to let go of any bitterness from the subsequent break-up and move on to a different path in life. Whether the relationship continues or not it must be realized that an intimate exchange will impact one's attitude and outlook. That's the influence intimacy brings.

## SELF DOUBT

*blaming others*
*on whom to depend*
*thinking positive*

Each passing day new challenges arise, sometimes a minor issue, sometimes of major proportion. No matter how difficult, or simple, each challenge will take time and effort. Hopefully, the effort then exerted gets the job done. When a job is well done there is a satisfying feeling, the greater the success the more a sense of accomplishment. As a matter of fact success followed by success reinforces self-confidence. Failure after failure, however, may cause frustration. In fact a sequence of failures may lead to self-doubt. What has happened is definitely damaging to the ego. Most are not really prepared for such a sordid sequence, thus there could come a feeling of 'losing it', a dread about no end of troubles. Such an experience, unfortunately, can happen at any time, anywhere. Alas, many times, when it happens, some believe others are the cause, in effect they blame others for their woes. The tendency is to vent the resulting feeling of frustration upon anyone nearby, whether family or acquaintance, innocent or not. But such an action likely creates more problems. A much better approach is to try and put your anger aside, to stay calm, and to face the unfortunate event. How you react to the situation is what really counts. Common sense tells you that it is better not to make matters worse. Thus it would be best to not let the setback go any further, but to rise instead to the challenge. It is a challenge which can be a character-building experience. True, mistakes likely will be made. But that's just part of the learning curve. The difficult part is that it is easier said than done, but the quicker the issue is resolved the less the feeling of frustration. Afterwards let it be said that you rose to the challenge.

Self-doubt can play havoc with the mind. Once it takes hold it can be a depressing experience. To make matters worse self-esteem tends to falter and become apparent to anyone who cares to notice. Thus you are vulnerable to taunts and ridicule. The natural inclination is to seek solitary comfort, withdrawing from society and away from people. Following the initial shock one often feels within a spark of hope, a fervour to overcome the turmoil within. Now is the moment to consider how the dilemma came about and a possible way out. Sometimes the doubter seeks an opinion from a trusted friend. Many times the advice is helpful, but, alas, not always. Furthermore, there is a possibility of being opened to criticism. Nevertheless it helps to tell someone, because by doing so there is released any pent-up rage, hostility and pain. What must be realized, the quicker the better, is that self-doubt cannot be overcome until one thinks positive. This requires one to seize any spark of hope kindled within and be positive in whatever one is doing. It doesn't matter what is done as long as you are openly flexible and willing to make constructive changes as you go along. Often sheer guts and determination are needed to do so. Whatever success is secured is then built upon for, hopefully, more success. In this manner self-confidence is restored within.

Anyone with self-doubt should consider, and be thankful for, the many advantages they presently enjoy and have. One such natural attribute is likely being free of ills and pain. This aspect to life usually is taken for granted, except by those sick and lame, individuals who are ailing and who would gladly give all their worldly possessions to be healthy - well, maybe not all but a portion of it. So keep in mind that the sick and lame are worse off than you. Incidentally, for those who are sick and lame self-doubt is the least of their problems. Likewise not to be overlooked, and thus considered, is having a sound mind. In today's society the actions of many seem to lack rhyme, reason or common sense. So be thankful for having a sound mind with your common sense intact. As a matter of fact wallowing in self pity seems narcissistic and not the cause of self-doubt. Let's face it, you have to rise, single-handedly, above any inkling feeling of low self-esteem. Often self-doubt is caused by letting others do what they want, such as to meddle in one's personal affairs with no resistance offered except words feebly spoken. Worse yet, if it was left up to the self-doubter to take action nothing would be done probably because she/he dreads making a mistake. However, this hesitant behaviour must be overcome. To do so one has to spend a meditative moment focusing on one's abilities and limitations. The objective of this focus now is to work within one's abilities and seek help whenever the issue is more than one's limitations. Any subsequent ensuing success ought to create an upbeat mood. You can create such an attitude by a simple project, namely by making neat and tidy, periodically, the environment you call home. Make that place echo with positive vibes. Very often this brings about a psychological lift to the spirit. In the process of doing these chores you will learn another positive trait - self-discipline. Now it is a matter of keeping a positive outlook in whatever you now do. Now is the time to boldly go where you timidly feared to venture before. But make no mistake, it is going to be a learning experience.

## PLANNING AHEAD

*be flexible*
*put it in writing*
*a personal accounting*

It can be disturbing to one's well being whenever a common day-to-day situation gets out of hand and starts to slide down a slippery slope. Nothing but chaos is anticipated thereafter. Naturally, turmoil stirs within. The trick is to stay calm and to correct the situation before it gets worse. After such an experience many resolve to do a bit of prior planning whenever possible. But, believe it or not, there are individuals who consider planning ahead to be a waste of time. They claim that unexpected glitches still occur. But that ought not to deter you from preparing a plan of action. Common sense says it's better to have a plan than none at all. What needs to be done is to be flexible during the actual execution for surprises and unexpected twists. The idea is to adjust to actual circumstances and, if necessary, to re-think the process. Likewise keep in mind that the actual end product might not turn out to be as anticipated. This is the difference between what was fantasized at the start and what really happened in the end.

For most people they commonly face each day with a rough idea of what has to be done then proceed to do what they can thereafter. Now and then a glitch might be encountered but often that is resolved without an issue. Some likewise will do a complex project with just a rough idea of what is desired overall. Surprisingly the outcome may turn out as expected. But sometimes it is started, done part way and then that would be it. For whatever reason the project is somehow abandoned. The hiatus status then tends to be permanent. In retrospect it probably would have been more prudent to sit down and do a bit of prior planning. It is far easier, for example, to move a wall, on paper, with an eraser than a wall of bricks, just laid, with a sledge hammer. Once pen is put to paper it becomes clearer whether or not what is desired is possible. If feasible then it is a matter of planning properly; tools necessary, materials required and the skills of others. Usually this takes more than one sitting because ideas and details tend to come on the spur of the moment. As a matter of fact it takes normally more time to plan properly than to do the actual work. With a plan of action in hand a complex project can be done in stages. More importantly, there is less likelihood of a project in hiatus cluttering the personal landscape.

As one matures and hopefully prospers there will come a time when one has to face a decision impacting significantly the path of one's future. Naturally, there is hesitancy. The mind is commonly flooded with a million worrisome questions. Still, one ought to be decisive. For sure, there is no use sitting down and moping. That won't resolve the issue. Here is where one should put pen to paper. Here is where the many puzzling questions are written down as they come to mind. You will be surprised but there will be a question, or more, which only you can decide the answer. Likewise there will be answers only time, or a decision taken, can tell. Still, by writing and analyzing the situation there will be less anxiety. Now one has to seek answers to the questions raised. This very likely entails a lot of reading, perhaps surfing the internet and seeking those knowledgeable in the subject matter. After considering all the information gained a reasonable decision can now be made. May circumstances and luck be in your favour.

## MEASURING SUCCESS

*the dream*
*one day at a time*
*with the least of effort*
*a matter of confidence*

What constitutes success commonly changes as one goes through life. In youthful years it probably is getting what is desired at the moment. In later years the dream of success might focus on a luxurious life style, possible a large home filled with creature comfort accoutrements. The dream of success hinges on what you want out of life. For some, this might be winning over others and winning again. On the other hand, for others, the concept of success is to live in peaceful harmony and loving kindness with everyone. What constitutes success is thus subjective and your concept of success likely differs from people you know. Such differing points of view are reflected in people's outlooks and attitudes. So the dream and fantasy for success can be an immediate wish or a life long search. As a matter of fact success achieved, or no longer pursued, brings, in turn, a new dream and fantasy. My suggestion is that you give a thought about what is success, from your perspective, and the consequences of that concept. Hopefully your dream is achievable within reason and respectable in the eyes of others. Sometimes, unfortunately, a person's dream of success may never come true.

How should one measure success ? Ordinarily it is pursued one task at a time, one goal to the next. Positive results may bring a sigh of relief, possibly a personal sense of accomplishment. After a few such results, success may be taken for granted and then become a reflex action in such situations. As for tasks out of the ordinary, there could be some trepidation, a hesitancy to proceed. Many times the task then is tackled with a hope and a prayer. Sometimes it works. Sometimes it doesn't. What should be done, at the onset, is to step back and consider how to do the task and any possible glitches. If there is any concern there might be sought a second opinion and, if need be, professional advice and help. Through such pursuits one learns about what they are able to do and when others should be consulted. The process is a confidence building activity. Unfortunately, some will not change their impulsive ways of doing things without giving any thought as to what is involved, no matter the tasks. The result, then, would either be a hit or a miss. Should you desire to increase the chance of success then step back beforehand and think the process through. By doing so your frame of mind may see potential drawbacks. Such conscious focus allows you to adjust to the actual situation as it happens. The key is that the task is being done with an open mind. In that respect hope for the best but, if anything, expect the worst.

To be successful is what many youths aspire to while they go through secondary schooling. They conjure up images of success in varied fields, perhaps sports or an esteemed academic pursuit or a career of fame and wealth. Transforming such a fantasy into a reality is a personal challenge. But it will take time and effort; talent certainly helps and, of course, determination. Alas, many, at this youthful stage of life, do their best only when compelled by circumstances or others. Often they go through each day doing the minimum with matching result. So success for them, unwittingly, is measured by just enough for the immediate moment. Unfortunately many maintain such a mentality even in adult life.

Another way to measure success, as previously mentioned, is one goal at a time. As a matter of fact, countless people measure success in a way most don't imagine. For instance, quite a few measure success just by merely staying alive. That's what those seriously sick do as they look forward to greeting each day, likewise the poor as they scrounge daily for something edible. Should they find a tasty scrap of food then success is theirs. A success no one can take from them. That ought to be the way success is measured, namely, in an incremental fashion, one set task at a time, from one progressive step to the next. Any obstacle encountered is a test of one's resolve. As obstacles are overcome, for better or for worse, one matures whether in self-confidence or in experience. The measure of success is that incremental gain in self confidence and experience. That's what the tortoise did to beat the hare.

## THE CHANGING SCENERY OF WORK

*no job is secure*
*finding a niche*
*taking the initiative*

People tend to follow a steady routine once they have a settled home life plus a regular job and income. But an abrupt end may come, without warning, to this pattern of comfort. A common disruptive event is job termination. Upon getting the upsetting news the cause, whether downsizing or otherwise, doesn't really matter because one's source of livelihood is now history, an unthinkable situation is now a reality. There is now experienced a sad sequence - a sinking feeling pervades the body, the emotions overwhelm the persona, the flood gates pent up within are ready to burst, rage may pour out willingly, depression normally sets in followed by self-doubt and maybe shame. Personal events seem to unfold for the worse. One's self-esteem sinks to a new low. So distressful can a job termination be that friends and acquaintances will, if they are able, stay away. So the now unemployed is shunned. Still, life goes on. The personal challenge now is how to face the coming days and weeks. What should be said to those one knows upon meeting them ? Furthermore, how can one now pay for one's way in life ? How can food be put on the dinner table ? What can one do about the incoming bills ? The reality of surviving now has to be faced. Ending this nightmarish scenario is not an easy challenge. With a little luck, and a lot of personal effort, another job can, hopefully, be found. To prepare for such a day, long beforehand, is a way to ease the emotional trauma and shock. Keep in mind that no job is secure. That is the likely reason why parents harp to their offsprings to study, study, study. Parents want to prepare them for the brave new world of adult life. Surely, in the opinion of many parents, with education and recognized credentials, a working niche ought to be easier to secure, especially after losing a job. To those who never listened, as a child, there is still time to study, albeit late, rather than never. After all, it is never too late to learn.

Finding a job is an economic opportunity which, during prosperous times, is easy to secure but, during frugal times, difficult to be had. It depends, of course, on who can supply the skills then in demand. So people tend to change jobs and careers as the economy shifts and dictates. But not everyone moves around job-wise. Some are satisfied with the job they have. They seem to accept the status they presently enjoy with equanimity. As each year passes they settle down into a routine including pursuing leisure, social merriment and, if so desired, having a family. Inevitably the job is an essential part of maintaining a life style. But this might not be good enough for quite a few. And so they will study, on their own time, for accredited training and more education. Alas, such a career path is so tedious and taxing that many will forego such studies, part way, never to resume. Nevertheless some will persist until the desired credential is achieved. As for those who stayed with the job at hand, they might progress up the corporate ladder as opportunity comes by. Occasionally some will speculate and wonder what if they had changed jobs and careers. Often those who so dream are weary about the uncertainty involved. Still, many do give a serious thought to such a change. As a matter of fact, one should sit down, occasionally, and reflect on the job situation. The reason why is because the business world is constantly shifting to a brave new scenario. Who knows, your present source of livelihood may soon be history for one reason or another: new technology, outsourcing, downsizing and other innovative steps. So you ought to prepare for such an event ever happening. You might need to pursue another line of work. True, there will be trying moments and maybe set backs, but unless you prepare, beforehand, then it can be difficult moving on at all. This is why you need to have a tentative plan in case your present job abruptly ends. Such a plan might involve a career path you always wanted to do but were not quite ready to pursue. But that is less likely to happen should there be no plan at all.

Bleak and desolate is the mind and outlook of someone who just lost a job. Alas, it happens every day. No economic group in society is spared, from clerical and blue collar workers to successful executives. But no matter how devastating this is to the one disenfranchised, the beat goes on in the rest of society. Being mired in self pity will likely douse, with anguish, any ray of hope that may spark within. Now is the time, however, to gather one's thoughts together and boldly seek new economic opportunity. This might come out of the blue and in a highly unlikely manner. It could arise from a chance encounter with someone mentioning a job opening or perhaps a potential career in a pioneering field. With determination and perseverance, plus luck, many do secure a new job and even another career. Naturally, there are no guarantees. What you ought to do, in general, is to assess your personal capability periodically, to ponder upon what you want to pursue and how to do so. Such an effort could be encapsulated into an updated resume, which is, by the way, useful in any job search. To some such an effort now might seem a waste but it serves as a periodic reminder about where you stand in the current job market. After all, the world is not going to come to your doorstep and offer a job to your liking. So you need to look out constantly for the opportune moment as it avails itself. The economy in society varies from country to country and, likewise, from one person to the next. The economy in society swings between prosperity and recession, even lower into depression. Incidentally, the difference between a recession and depression, from a personal point of view, is a matter of perspective - a recession is the case of someone you know losing a job while a depression means you are the one out of a job. Recession and depression are now common phenomena. Be prepared.


## GETTING UPSET

*the only 'right' way*
*who gains, who loses*
*that was no oversight*


There is a touch of idiosyncrasy in each of us. It seems to stem from a personal habitual reaction, usually unique, to a certain set of circumstances. It can be so habitual that one's reaction can become an identifying trait. What seems to bring this about is the fact that each of us marches to the beat of a different drummer. So we tend to do some actions similar to others and some actions in a somewhat unique and personal way. In spite of this there are individuals who want to impose their way of doing things upon others. That, to them, is the only 'right' way. That may be an imperative rule for certain specific situations but, surely, not for every activity. What ought to be considered is the final outcome and the end result achieved, not how, in general, an individual personally gets there. Still, some people become upset should others not follow their instructions to the letter.

The crux of the matter is that they are not really concerned about the end result, rather it reflects a personal desire for total control. What those who impose their will on others ought to keep in mind is that everyone, if given a chance to do so, may do things differently. This natural trait ought to be respected as long as the desired objectives and end results are achieved. Should you be on the receiving end of such an imposing situation then it is now a matter of letting the one controlling know that you are aware of the nit-picking interest shown and why. What happens thereafter is another story. But, at least, you let them know that you know why they do what they do.

It is said that no two individuals think alike. That I can believe whenever I see someone doing something clumsily and crudely. I likewise believe that two persons can execute the same action but for two differing reasons. Furthermore, strange as it sounds, sometimes people act with the best of intentions but invariably cause an adverse impact. On the other hand, people may act out of malice only to create a beneficial outcome. So should someone somehow offend you, don't jump to the conclusion that it was intentional. Confront the individual about the apparent offense and hear what she/he has to say. No use getting upset and angry over an accidental event. Thus, in general, accept the actions of others with an open mind. At the same time, go beyond the spoken word and keep an enquiring mind. Finally, focus on who stands to gain and who will likely pay for any gain. If that seems eccentric then so be it.

In dealing with others, whether at work or for a social effort or voluntary cause, it is common to become involved in a team. The natural tendency is to be cooperative and trusting - more so should the venture be far reaching such as a task force or a charitable drive. But, unfortunately, not everyone involved might be willing to be truly cooperative and trusting. So, for one reason or another, there could be a 'misunderstanding' causing a rift between someone on the team and you. Should you firmly believe that you did no wrong, it can be upsetting. It can be so upsetting that you may lose your cool, so disturbing there is an urge to yell and scream. But such an emotional outburst could lead to dire consequences, perhaps a divisive parting of the ways. So before that happens you might decide to resolve the issue through dialogue. By doing so you intend to make clear where you stand and what's expected in the future. But whatever takes place next, doubt now creeps into the relationship. Sadly, for resolution of such matters, some people are not willing to admit any personal blame even though they are at fault. Worse yet, they might have no respect for those they dislike and act accordingly. This may result in another 'misunderstanding'. What this could bring about, in the mind of the victim, is a personal hesitancy and a lack of confidence in the relationship. This is a situation you might find yourself in. Look out for a third occurrence which only validates that it was not an oversight in the first instance. Getting upset will not, therefore, make a difference. Either lessen your involvement or bid adieu. Consider the fiasco as a learning experience in your journey through life. Next time try not to be so trusting and gullible.

## BEING POSITIVE

*part of the problem*
*life goes on*
*having a sense of humour*

In whatever one pursues there are hopes, expectations and maybe wishful thinking. Such desires might be realistic or a fantasy. A realistic possibility depends on one's efforts, actual circumstances as well as the actions and reactions of anyone else involved. The attitudes of those involved can play a vital role. Taking a negative attitude, for example, may focus a person's thoughts mostly on what could go wrong. In the process negative energy may bring about a self-fulfilling prophecy. On the other hand a positive attitude likely creates a constructive outlook, thus one takes setbacks in stride while helping to find a solution. Needless to say circumstances may be such that no matter what action is taken the outcome will be less than expected. Sometimes a pursuit involves a common cause with others. Often, in such instances, people will notice a troublesome situation but limit any involvement to being a bystander just offering, if anything, verbal criticism. It is as if it's not their problem to resolve. It is almost as if they don't believe that their involvement make the difference to success. But, who knows, that very well could be the difference. It is a matter of being proactive and **not be part of the problem, but be part of the solution**.

Living with others leads to relationships with many - the immediate and extended family, friends, even foes, plus associates at work, not to mention management and clientele. At times the interaction is pleasant and simple. But at times it can be taut and tense, even at crossed purposes. As a matter of fact in any long term relationship there will invariably, often inevitably, be hassles and differences. In other words, the action taken by one party will not be to the liking of the other. Likewise, for one reason or another, conflicts will occur as each pursues a personal agenda. After all, it is natural for each and everyone to look out for their own personal interest and welfare. Surprisingly overlooked is the occasional personal tendency, hopefully rare, for paranoid behaviour with the mistaken belief that everyone else is against them. In any case there will be, now and then, weird and wacky behaviour from each party of the relationship. So it is a matter of one accepting odd behaviour to be out of the ordinary and thus tolerable. As a matter of fact most accept such an occasional, out of the ordinary occurrence without thinking much about it. Just be sure not to have tunnel vision that your way is the only way, for there very likely are other ways to get the same job done. Besides what really matters is the eventual outcome. Finally, a positive attitude, believe it or not, is to accept the outcome irrespective of whether it is a success or a setback. Each and every outcome, success or setback, is merely a temporary event in an established relationship. Accept we should for life goes on regardless.

A common social phenomenon is frustration. Frustration causes many to feel emotionally down and believing their dreams, even hopes, are now smashed to smithereens. What invades the mind is the introspective thought - 'Why me ?' That's the question pondered, a question possibly reflecting a subconscious plea for sympathy. Often this assumes that no one else could be worse off. But that, as you are probably aware, is highly unlikely. What to do next ? Any possible action seems fraught with shortcomings and no totally redeeming answer. Still, one must move beyond just moping and brooding. What must be personally accepted and recognized is that no gain can be made by doing nothing. What must be done is to proactively consider all possible options and put into action the one seemingly most appropriate. This must be done before the opportunity of doing anything passes. Often what's done is to follow one's gut feeling. Well, that's better than just moping and brooding. The key is to do whatever is humanly possible. At least one tried. If only there was a natural antidote for stress - actually there is. It is called laughter which, in the opinion of many, is the best medicine - laugh and the world laughs with you, not at you. So all one needs to do is to partake of laughter. And how, pray tell, is that swallowed? Well, that's easy, what is required is a sense of humour. By the way, a sense of humour is inherent in all of us. This is the trait that instinctively sees humour whenever irony occurs in a tense situation, or when someone makes an error in judgement or slips down without warning. With a sense of humour you can be positive in your thinking. With a sense of humour you are better prepared for whatever the outcome, success or setback, of any endeavour. So be prepared as there will be more challenging moments on the horizon.

## GIVE AND TAKE

*taking ownership*
*giving a helping hand*
*getting along*

Whatever we do usually entails our own self-interest and personal welfare. Hardly ever is it done with the intention of harming anyone. But, now and then, that is precisely what happens. Fortunately, in many instances, the harm done is of no significance thus a sincere apology will often suffice. In a few instances, however, there could be actual harm, perhaps even of a psychological nature. How does one take ownership then ? That is an ethical question only the perpetrator can answer. Who knows, there may be genuine fear that the victim will exact revenge. As to whether an apology or more will suffice only the victim can say. Should none be forthcoming then some victims are convinced, in their heart, that what goes around will come around. When that happens the empty feeling of futility the victim now felt will be experienced by the perpetrator. That is the hope of some victims. As for any insulting action, whether intended or not, ownership can, in most cases, help the victim to cope. It is about social ethics and personal honour, not to mention common courtesy. More importantly, by admitting the deed there is, as far as some are concerned, bestowed a clear conscience. Admitting to committing the act is, of course, a personal choice. But it certainly helps the peace of mind of both parties.

Co-existing with others is a social phenomenon which begins the moment we emerge forth into this world. Our first relationship usually is with the most influential person in each of our lives - our loving mom. Relationships thereafter expand to the immediate and extended family, with acquaintances, often from school, followed by work and, all along, others of like interests. Each relationship has its own boundaries and parameters. All are far from perfect. So rarely is a relationship totally satisfactory; sometimes one gains, sometimes one gives. Each relationship tends to have its own issues, even rules of conduct. How a relationship evolves depends on one's needs and wants. Quite a few relationships eventually lead to friendship with happy moments, maybe disappointing times, perhaps misunderstandings. Seldom is it recorded who gains and who gives willingly. Such is the joy of friendship and fellowship. Hardly ever is something expected in return. Giving from the heart tends to bring a joy of its own. That's what awaits those who help others in dire need. If the offered help is declined, well, accept the refusal in good faith. On the other hand if you truly need help why not ask ? You likely will be surprised how willing others are to help. Let's co-exist with a willingness to help each other.

Each brand new day finds people working everywhere. They work sometimes alone and sometimes in conjunction with others. Those that work closely together understand the need to complement each other's efforts to get the task done. Give and take, for them, is a normal component of the job. As for those who work alone, there are usually working associates nearby although the task at hand is just for them to do. For situations out of the ordinary, they very likely go to those supervising to jointly decide what to do. But there are times when it is left up to those working alone to solely resolve the matter. What is then done might work, but it might not. A second opinion, before starting, could be of help. What should be considered is the resource readily at hand, namely, colleagues nearby. Here is a knowledgeable group familiar with the protocols and who might have encountered a similar situation before. Their opinion is there merely for the asking. But there are individuals who will not consult their colleagues, seemingly preferring, instead, to work in splendid isolation. Why such alienation is a tough question. Many times it is due to a hard-line self-centered persona with a belief that their way is the only way. As most are aware, rarely is this so. Worse yet, this hard-line persona often displays a tough exterior while dealing with others. Anyone with common sense knows that while dealing with others it helps to have a 'give-and-take' latitude as well as discretion. This is what it takes to get along. To do so takes an open mind. In this respect commingling and fellowship certainly augments one's interactions with working associates. This also promotes good will within the working environment.

## CLUTTERS OF THE MIND

*a feeling of well-being*
*high expectations*
*setting goals*
*resisting change*

To be hale and hearty is certainly one aspect to well being. Many, in that respect, are content just to be free of any ailments and illnesses. Some are willing to go one better by strenuously exercising. But well-being goes beyond a healthy bodily frame. Well-being also entails peace of mind. In this troublesome and hectic world such a state of mind seems hard to encounter. Still, that should not stop anyone from trying. Peace of mind tends to come sporadically with moments of tranquility. This may happen, by chance, whenever one solitarily sits down, bare bottom, doing what comes naturally. If that brings a moment of peace then enjoy the moment. As a matter of fact many put this peaceful pause to use. This might be, for instance, to consider how to resolve a pressing personal issue. Clearing such clutter from the mind helps, for sure, one's well-being. Of course, it would be better not to have such clutter in the first place. Alas, creating clutters within the mind is a common phenomenon. Clutters often unnecessarily created are: having high *expectations*; setting *goals* for others; and resisting *change*. Resist creating such clutters and there is greater hope for personal well-being.

High expectation is a natural human desire in whatever we do. It is what motivates most of us at the start of an endeavour. Unfortunately, in many cases, high expectation is more a fantasy than a reality. This ought to be kept in mind in whatever one pursues. Be aware also that there will be individuals who will not leave the outcome solely to fate and circumstances. So they try to manipulate the situation, by hook or by crook, to abet their personal cause, even if they have to plot and scheme nefariously. [Trust you have already identified any such characters within your social circle] Often others participate innocently and unknowingly, maybe unwillingly. But once the subterfuge is discerned the outcome will probably be to no-one's satisfaction. Such outcomes have happened and seem to be the origin for the expression **hope for the best but expect the worst**. So be prepared for such a possibility whenever others are involved in whatever you do. By doing so the high expectations at the start will not become a frustrating experience in the end.

As we go through life we gain valuable experience and meaningful insights about human nature. Errors, omissions and misguided intentions sprinkle our path of learning. Occasionally we encounter and become involved with someone who seemed sincere and well intentioned. But eventually, in some cases, we walk away disillusioned. Such experience underlines how naive and innocent we once were. This motivates many to tell about such pitfalls to those, usually younger, less experienced and whom they like, how to steer clear of such errors and omissions. Some become self-appointed mentors for the younger persons. So they establish set *goals* and personal objectives for their newly designated wards, much like what a parent will do for an offspring. How these wards react will likely differ. Some cooperate willingly and some reluctantly. Sometimes they reluctantly go along with the plan. Others, however, may object, even, perhaps, oppose the whole process. How a mentor responds to a reaction less than willing is what counts. Quite a few may demand nothing less than full cooperation. After all, it is being done with the best of intentions, and for the welfare of the younger ward. But such a stance is a one-sided affair. Such a stance fails to recognize, much less consider, the wish, much less the say, of the individual who counts the most, namely, the person whose future is being shaped and moulded. Surely, the final word must be theirs. True, in spite of objections there can be constructive progress and success. But how long this will last now seems questionable. Success can be enhanced should there be a mutual and willing involvement from the start. This requires the beneficiary to commit the mind, the heart and the will totally to the process. Otherwise frustration creeps into the scenario before even a step is taken. That is exactly what no one wants. That is what setting goals arbitrarily for others can bring about. In other words, goals are best achieved should there be total commitment from the start.

The beauty of a customary routine is its familiarity. Such familiarity brings, for most, a high level of comfort. In contrast is the trepidation that we feel with a situation involving *change*. The natural tendency is to resist. This resistance likely stems from a fear of the unknown, from the uncertainty of what is to come. What you should ponder upon, for a moment, is what you have observed and noticed for the past month if not the past year. Reflect upon the fact that, as time passes, your personal sphere of influence and worldly environment underwent a degree of change, sometimes for the better, sometimes for the worse, but inevitably there is change. So change happens whether one likes it or not. It seems better, therefore, for one's well being, to adapt to what is going to be new at the start, to do more than hope for the best and expect the worst. In fact, a receptive attitude can help the process. Change is a situation somewhat akin to breaking a bottle. Now the broken pieces of hope must be picked up, sorted, and a new personal order put into place. One has to move on. That's life. Living solely in the past is no way to help one's well-being, but moving on and adapting may very well help. So be prepared and ready for change. Try to accept this willingly and with an open mind.

## LIVING LIFE TO THE FULL

*the temperamental factor*
*decisions, decisions, decisions*
*what will be, will be*
*facing a brave new world*

The ways of human nature are unpredictable. One moment a person's action may be with reason and logic, but the next minute the action displayed can be irrational and emotional. Similarly, joy and laughter may fill the air one minute but melancholy may follow the next second. Such are the volatile vagaries of human emotions which can play havoc with a person's action. It may stem from a psychic reverberation of what others are thinking, or a gut feeling of what others around have in mind, or an instinctive read of what is going to happen. Should the vibe be intimidating the impulse seems to be for one to respond emotionally, perhaps violently. The humane challenge is to remain calm, to bridle the innate rage, to smooth any ruffled feathers of hate until the feeling of rage takes flight. To do otherwise is to invite trouble. It is advisable to step back and allay your frayed nerves. To incite a fight is to deepen any divide and escalate the dispute. No good can come of that. Incidentally, people say that the best form of defense is offense. But striking first is a proactive move unilateral in action and without adequate justification. The result is uncalled-for enmity. Ill-will commonly begets ill-will, not to mention the bitter after-taste created. But please don't throttle the passionate zeal which comes with emotions. Such zeal can be a constructive force. It is a matter of putting the zeal into humane pursuits. By doing so the personal zest for life can only increase for the better.

In some societies of old a woman had no say about whom she married. That's decided, for her, by her parents. A lady of the modern era probably shudders at the thought of this. How can a woman be happy with such an arrangement ? Fortunately, a lady of today decides, for herself, whom to marry. Will this guarantee happiness ? Hell, no. We all know people who are either divorced or separated or even unhappy with their present married life. This underlies how far-reaching are the consequences of an important decision. But, of course, not all decisions are that unforgiving. Each morning we awake to thereafter make, as the day progresses, decision after decision. Most times it's simple - what to wear, where to eat, and so on. Occasionally a decision will take time to make. When we do so will depend on the situation and surrounding circumstances. Sometimes the issues involved are straightforward and a decision easily follows. Sometimes more information is needed to make one. Then there are times when a decision is not made until the last possible minute. Occasionally we may wait too long and, as a result, someone else seized the opportunity or, perhaps, circumstances changed. In other words, the decision chosen was to do nothing and so the opportunity to do anything was lost. That's how important it is to make your mind up within a reasonable time. So be prepared to be decisive in whatever you do.

Uncertainty, now and then, is strewn along our path of the future. It's unavoidable whenever there is change. To counteract any chaotic impact many try to anticipate any snag and plan accordingly. But, of course, not every possible outcome can be anticipated. At times the outcome that unfolds is a surprise and has an unexpected twist. A pleasant surprise is welcome and often greeted with a smile. On the other hand a setback tends to be a disappointment. In a few instances it is met with denial. But to remain in denial is certainly not going to help. What needs to be done is to accept a fact that's dismal as a reality. Until that is done only grief can follow. In fairness to any hesitancy it is natural to ponder what to do with an outcome less than anticipated. Nevertheless no good can come about until the situation is rectified. Let's face it, there is a fear that the situation can get worse should anything be attempted. But act one must. Fortunately many setbacks, once tackled, are quickly resolved. But sometimes it becomes a learning experience. One has very little choice but to proceed and try the best one can while hoping it works. Sometimes it is a matter of trial and error. Measure success one progressive step at a time. Perhaps what you desired is not to be. "Qué será, será". What will be, will be.

Life is both simple and complex. Every action we take is a simple event, but the alternate actions possible, as well as reactions, are complex in comparison. Many times what seems simple is complex to do. Similarly, what seems complex is often, done step by step, simple to achieve. Acquiring peace of mind likewise seems a complex state to achieve but it is really simple to gain. It is a matter of seeking peace of mind in whatever we do. Any action we take, which is disturbingly malevolent, disturbs the mind too. So listen to the intuitive urging of the mind. Whenever possible step back and reflect on what life is all about. Likewise enjoy, when you can, a peaceful pause amid nature. Such is the joy, for instance, that can be felt viewing a sunset. Everywhere, within sight, seems to be a part of one's being. Every sound complements the moment. It is as if one has merged with the landscape and is in unity with the universe. Alas, the joy quickly fades as we rejoin society in progress. The moment rapidly vaporizes as the mind once more focuses on earthly man-made situations. Try to retain the calmness of the peaceful pause particularly if you encounter aggression and intrusiveness. As to the complex and simple aspects to life, keep whatever you do simple and the complex sequences will be less complicated for you.

*Supplements*

# Supplement A - Communicating

*personal gain*
*a two way process*
*it might take three different ways*

People, here, there, everywhere - some we like, some we don't, most we don't know. Each day we communicate with a few of them; greeting these few, making small talk, telling them our opinions, maybe expressing our thoughts and feelings. Sometimes we say something surprisingly new to them. Sometimes we, in turn, learn. Now and then we gain a different, often new, point of view. As a result, we increase our personal understanding and knowledge.

Communicating is a two way process. It involves someone speaking and another one listening. At times we tend to overlook that a word spoken to us could have an intended meaning different from what comes to our mind. Take, for example, a simple answer **yes**. This might imply one of the following meaning:

I agree

I understand what you are saying

That's your viewpoint, but mine may be different

Please stop talking

Now it's my turn to speak

Yet when we hear **yes**, we usually presume that the listener is agreeing with what we say - completely, totally, one hundred percent. Another common assumption seems to be a tacit agreement, on the other party's part, with the reason we have in mind. But, alas, this may not be so. It's similar to a situation where a thousand people voted for the same candidate but for a thousand DIFFERENT reasons. So please don't make the mistake of taking a  **yes**  answer to imply total agreement with your point of view.

Talking, or getting the message across, is the easy part in communicating. The difficult part is to ascertain whether or not the listener really understood what you meant. Should the listener seem puzzled, then your message - like a spaceship gone astray - may not have landed. Repeating what you said, with the same words, may still cause a puzzled stare. If this be the case then try telling the same message using new and different words. Someone once told me that a message may have to be told at least three different ways before a listener understands what was meant.

# PUT IT IN WRITING

*a case of presumption*
*a message of importance*

Here is a scene of miscommunication familiar to all of us; it may happen at work or it may happen at home. You are in the middle of a difficult task when something else pressing demands your urgent attention. So, due to the circumstances, you hurriedly tell someone nearby, maybe a co-worker or relative, what to do before focusing on the urgent matter. But upon returning to the task you find out, to your horror, that what was done is not what you had in mind. This shows how an action which seems plain and straight forward, to you, might not be so to others. So common is this occurrence you would think others surely would do better. Alas, they have yet to learn your intuitive ways.

Sometimes what we say differs from what we have in mind. It is as if what we uttered was done without due consideration for the words as spoken. Often, however, it is difficult putting into words one's innermost thoughts. And so for a message of importance one ought to pause and reflect on the words, phrases and sentences within the message made. Of course, the message must include information relevant to special instructions, precautions and explanations. As a matter of fact it might help to first jot down whatever comes to mind. The very act of writing it down tends to make us think in a logical train of thought. But don't stop there, also read over what was written. Finally, once you have finished writing, time permitting, let it sit then read what you wrote much later, preferably the following day. You should check what's written with a fresh mind. After all, if something is worthwhile doing, it is worthwhile doing well.

## ABOUT YOUR LISTENERS

*the comfort of talking at home*

The art of communicating is learnt, by most, in the setting of the home. Communicating at home can so familiar that a listener can practically finish a sentence another in the family started. So the words spoken are easily understood as to the intended meaning. Once one ventures outside of the home, however, it is a different story. It can be problematic as to clarity thus understanding and meaning could be an issue. So you ought to have an attentive ear and eyes to interpret the response of the listener. The response in words and body language tells how the message was received. Unfortunately some people refuse to pay attention to how a listener responds. Their attitude seems to be focused on just their own concern without due consideration for the other party. Of course, should the other party find what's said to be unacceptable there is likely a need to discuss and, hopefully, come to an understanding. It is important, therefore, to employ words, phrases and colloquial expression common in use.

# BODY LANGUAGE

*telling it as it is*

Communicating goes beyond the spoken word. What is said might differ from what the speaker has in mind. That is where body language counts. The next chance you get just take a closer look at the body language of a person who is on top of the world or someone burdened with woes. Here is an opportunity to employ one's power of observation. Often a person's emotional make-up, regardless of what they say, is revealed uncannily through body language especially the glint of the eyes. So try and focus your attention on the body language of others while conversing with them. Try and correlate tone of voice with body language for the many various moods - being uncomfortable, happy, sad or experiencing a moment of delight. Most people usually signal their true feelings through body language. But often we let our minds override this signal by what a person says. Surely, we are not being deceived ? Here is where you ought to trust your instinctive read of body language. So be attentive to the signals given by voice and body language. Keep in mind that a similar signal is given whenever we tell a lie. So think twice about misleading others by what you say. *A word to the wise is sufficient.*

## APPEARANCE

*image counts*
*judging by appearance*
*an opinion of character*

At one stage of my life I usually spent my Saturday mornings sleeping late. But once awake I jumped out of bed, washed my face, put on some comfortable old clothes, and went about my personal chores including going to the market, store and mall. After many such mornings I confronted myself, perchance, in a public mirror. I was flabbergasted by the image I saw - unshaven, hair disarrayed and dressed like a bum. Surely, that is NOT me, yours truly, in the mirror! What I thought of myself was quite different from the character depicted in the mirror. My self esteem fell to an all-time low. The image I discerned seems to be a likely candidate for the mental case of the year. This brought home, to me, a realization that one ought to glance, occasionally, in the mirror so as to reinforce one's self-confidence about the image being projected through appearance. It also brought home a greater understanding of the phrase - *first impressions are lasting impressions.*

At this moment the way you look, from head to toe and currently attired, conveys a certain image. It might be positive or, hopefully, neutral. Expensive clothes tend to impress. Good looks are definitely a natural asset. But not all of us can afford expensive clothes nor are blessed with natural good looks. Still, a clean and neat appearance commonly projects a friendly and positive image. We seem to form an impression of others, just by appearance, from an early age. I can remember how a bunch of us preteen schoolers judged the mood of our headmistress by the outfit she wore. Each dress, in our opinion, erroneously or not, reflected her mood for that day - green for pleasant, yellow for terror, and so on. In much the same manner people tend to judge others just by their appearance. The dress code of today may be relaxed but it still counts to be presentable. At least one ought to be appropriately dressed so that friends will not be uncomfortable being seen with you. My suggestion is to check yourself in the mirror before stepping forth from home. The image seen ought not to be such that others, especially children, are apprehensive about shaking your hand.

A common human trait is to take the initial visual impression of a person and formulate an immediate opinion of her/his character. But the character visualized likely will differ from the impression once you make their acquaintance. In the process, you might be surprised by how misleading appearance can be. Yes, first impression is a lasting one, but it can be erroneous. So don't be too hasty in judging the action of others only by what you observe. Try and get to know the person within before passing judgement particularly on the intent of any action they take.

## TOTALLY DIFFERENT PEOPLE

*going beyond the visual image*
*honesty is the best policy*

Venturing forth into a new environment, such as a strange venue, makes many tense, perhaps nervous. More than likely this comes about from not knowing what to expect. Talking with a stranger often falls within this category, perhaps for both parties. So whatever can be done to lessen the tension helps. In that respect being presentable in appearance is a plus. Also helpful is a pleasant voice with words spoken clearly and simply. But what can cause concern, as a listener, is a noticeably heavy accent with pronunciation differing from what you expect. In such cases one likely has no choice but to request a repeat of what was said so as to ensure there is no misunderstanding. If need be, tell in your own words what you believe was said. In turn, should there be a puzzled look by the other party, then repeat whatever you said but using new and different words. Finally, the aspect which counts most in communicating with others has nothing to do with talking. It is about listening. Many people, alas, tend to ignore most of what the other party is saying. In other words, they fail to be attentive listeners. Hope that you are not one of them.

Once in a blue moon you might need to communicate in depth with someone new and totally different - strange speech patterns, exotic dress code, maybe a distant culture. You may truly be at the limits of your patience while conversing. Speak about challenging moments, here is one. In such an instance just talk the way you customarily do. Should it appear that the other party has some difficulty understanding what you say, then talk slowly and clearly using simple words. Try also to read their body language and responding tone. Keep in mind that certain words may have a meaning and connotation different to them. Whatever you say, please try and be diplomatic. In addition, don't overlook the possibility that they could be familiar with your language and culture. After all, this might be learnt from the media such as radio and television. So, whatever you say, be sincere and honest.

## SPEAKING TO AN AUDIENCE

*focus on what you want to say*

Speaking to a large audience of people tends to create anxiety no matter how experience a speaker may be. As for doing so for the first time, it can be terrifying. Anxiety shows its nasty form in many ways - a dry throat, a tense sensation, a momentarily loss of words or perhaps a nervous twitch. Such symptoms are common even for those have addressed an audience in the past. Otherwise anxiety could make you become self-conscious. Don't be afraid of the staring eyes from the audience. To combat such anxiety try and focus just on what you are going to say. Naturally, what helps is to prepare beforehand. Some even rehearse what will be said in front of a mirror. Once you are on stage then speaking to the audience is somewhat akin to thinking out loud. As a matter of fact many speakers, once they get going, don't know when to stop. It is almost as if they are hypnotized by the sound of their own voice. To prevent this happening to you, try not to repeat whatever is said. In addition, set a time limit on your speech. It may help by wearing a watch with a beeper. Another way is to get a friend to signal you. A common signal, used for live shows, is for the friend to run the index finger across her/his throat signaling to 'cut' talking. With a little luck the audience will clap. Who knows why, maybe it is because you have finished talking ! Afterwards a few of them may tell you that they like your speech. Take what they say with a grain of humour.

## SPEAKING IN ANGER

*an upsetting scenario*

Anger - that dark raging force of ill-will that knows no bounds, a flaming genie uncorked from a psyche bottle. In most instances it is an upsetting action by others which triggers this emotional outburst. It could be precipitated by a sarcastic remark or perhaps an apparent spiteful action. In any case anything you say in anger usually is not readily taken as important even if it is meaningful and logical. Anyone within shouting distance will, momentarily, be taken aback as they look, maybe agape, at your gyration and violent action. The outcome of your outburst is that you may be labeled a hothead, an unstable character, even though you might be in the right. In other words, the less one says in anger, the better. Treat such a situation as a test of self-control. Before saying anything, take a deep breath and breathe out slowly. Repeat this breathing exercise at least four times. Hopefully, by then, you will have regained your composure and clarity of mind. If you once more feel anger boiling within, then you must walk away without uttering another word. At this point in time you are not thinking, or talking, in a logical and rational manner. So try to vacate the contaminating environment even in the face of derisive laughter. An ill-advice I have heard given, for such a situation, is **don't get mad, get even**. Even this ought to be done in a calm and collective manner thus, naturally, at a later time and date.

## SPEAKING WITH BACKGROUND NOISE

*always a challenge*

At times speaking to others, especially an audience, happens in less than ideal conditions. A common interference comes from background noise such as a nearby boom box or table talk chatter. The usual impulse is to ignore the issue, recite hastily what one wants to say, breathe a sigh of relief, then step away from the limelight. But think for a moment, how was your message received by the listening audience ? To address the interference some speakers acknowledge openly the disturbance in a jovial manner and to beseech the forbearance of the audience. Usually this tends to make those listening sympathetic and thus more attentive. As for the speech given, it helps to have a close friend hear, beforehand, what you intend to say. Such a rehearsal allows constructive comment and more effective impact. Keep in mind, however, that not everyone in the audience may want to listen.

## FEEDBACK

*an attentive eye*

In any endeavour there is a human desire to attain a certain result. In that respect there usually is a desire likewise to determine the degree of success achieved. The same can be said about giving a speech. A conscientious speaker appreciates knowing this impact. A common feedback, on this issue, is how the audience reacts after the speech. A laudable oration is greeted with applause and favourable comments. On the other hand a lukewarm response, or less, is what awaits a poorly given speech. Better yet, it would be nice to know how the audience is responding while one is talking. To do so one has to have a keen observing eye on the audience while speaking. One has to glance at the panorama of people and discern, overall, their reaction by monitoring the movement of their eyes and body language. If they are, in general, attentive and quiet then that is a hopeful sign. However, should quite a few be engrossed in table talk and walking about then it is, unfortunately, time for brevity in whatever else one has to say. Evidently you are drifting away from what is interesting to the audience. As a matter of fact in deciding, beforehand, what is to be said there ought to be foremost in mind the interest of the audience. That is the perspective which makes a speech worthwhile hearing. If there is any uncertainty then get a second opinion, prior to your presentation, from a close friend about what you tentatively plan to say.

## LISTENING

*personal manners*

Most times people have no difficulty telling what they have in mind. At the same time many have difficulty listening to all of what you would like to say. I once was like that. Even now I have to consciously remind myself to restrain from finishing a sentence another person starts. I ought to let others say what they want before uttering a single word. Courtesy and proper etiquette should have been shown. At one time I also would voice any disagreement in the middle of their discourse. How crude and rude. Cordiality and consideration ought to be observed. Come to think of it, I commonly got angry whenever someone wouldn't let me finish whatever I had to say. So interrupting others who are speaking is not courteous. Mea culpa. I have changed. Now I let others finish speaking before saying a word, even if I disagree with what they are saying. You will be surprised what commonly happens whenever you allow someone to finish speaking before saying a word. There is a lull. Perhaps they are curious about whether or not you are listening ! The lull is your chance to say your piece. Hopefully, they let you do so. The key to being an effective speaker seems also to be a patient listener. Trust that you have such patience.

## HEARSAY

*Mary had a little lamb*

Hearing others talk about their personal accomplishments and troubles can be boring. But once they change the subject to current gossip, especially about someone you know, then it transforms into an interesting topic. Whether the gossip is true or not many seem eager to spread any demeaning gossip. As a matter of fact it tends to be distorted, for the worse, from one pair of lips to the next. It is much like what can happen, through gossiping, to a statement as simple as **Mary had a little lamb**. As this story circulates, each person may exaggerate the statement a wee bit. By the time the statement reaches the original teller of tale it could become **Mary is a black sheep**. So keep in mind that hearsay is likely an unproven blotch on someone's character that serves no good purpose. By repeating, it, however, you are adding credence to that blotch. If you absolutely must say something then at least state, before you start, that it is strictly hearsay and not first-hand information. But it is more humane and considerate not to mention it at all. Throttle the thought of being a bearer of scandalous rumour.

# CYBERSPACE AND THE INTERNET

*no face to face interaction*

With each passing day there seems to be a new electronic device on the market. Often computerized,sometimes digitalized. Now we can traverse afar through cyberspace no matter what's the hour. So user friendly is cyberspace we tend to react spontaneously. Now, without hesitation, we can tell the other party what we think and feel. But such impulsive behaviour has its consequences. Once a message enters cyberspace it is, for all intent and purpose, permanent. Even when there is a change of heart. Worse yet, confidential information is no longer a secret. Such concerns are a good reason why we need to know, beforehand, how trustworthy is the other party. Alas, many presume such confidence from the start although the other party could be a total stranger. A good rule of thumb is to step away from the laptop whenever there is angry or vindictive sentiment. A similar rule is to question why certain personal information is being asked. Whatever you decide to do it seems prudent to err on the side of caution. So keep this in mind whenever communicating in cyberspace.

## Supplement B - Communicating At Work

*T. G. I. F.*
*the active spending of time*

For most people their work is the source, and the means, for the lifestyle they enjoy. As for those working, about only a handful in a hundred may enjoy the work they do. For the rest work is commonly filled each week with low expectations. Get up on Monday morning often slow and reluctant. Dress, maybe in an indifferent manner, and, after a set morning routine, arrive at the workplace. Put in a seemingly never-ending first day. Get back home tired but now have to do personal chores perhaps preparing supper. Afterwards try to relax for a while before sleeping. More of the same on Tuesday. Feel fatigued by Wednesday. Experience more fatigue and perhaps boredom by Thursday. Feel no better on Friday but now look forward to the break away from work. T. G. I. F. [Thank goodness it's Friday] Weekend, ready or not, here you come. Soon you will be on your own time and away from the drudgery of work.

Practically all feel that they are truly accountable to no one on how they spend their time. Well, here is a simple accounting query, where did you spend most of your hours actively awake last week? For many, without question, it was at work. As a matter of fact here is where people spent the bulk of their time awake year in, year out. Yet here is the place most hardly give a thought about communicating clearly and effectively. Even though here is where communication commonly is the root cause of many misunderstandings including well-meaning intentions. Here is where people ignore the opinions, even valid comments, of close associates. Surely, here is where one ought to try and communicate as well as possible. Doing so ensures less vexations, perhaps unnecessary work, such as a task being done a second time. Effective communication in the work arena might create a positive and constructive environment. More importantly, doing so very likely will lower the stress levels of each and all.

## READING THE MANAGER'S MIND

*the power of hindsight*
*being blamed*
*the backlog*

Staff who have been on the job for quite a while know how to get routine work done - what to do, how to do it and the result to be expected. For work out of the ordinary, however, they ought to be given as much detail as possible including what's expected of them and the results anticipated. But once in a while a supervisor doesn't say much. It seems as if the boss is not quite sure about what to do but wants a specific job done without telling how. Whether this is the case or not staff often are willing to try and do what they think is appropriate. So they proceed with the best of intentions. However the outcome might not be to the liking of the boss. Naturally, the boss is going to be disappointed. How this disappointment is expressed might affect the morale of staff. Believe it or not, there are supervisory personnel who will accept such an outcome with equanimity. However, there will likely be many more who will distance themselves from failures. These, with the knowledge of hindsight, will comment on what should have been done. Evidently, what is so obvious to the boss is not apparent to staff. Another case of workers not having the uncanny ability to read the mind of the boss. After all, they have worked together for so long that should not be a problem. Maybe managers can read the mind of others ? I doubt it. Yet such blame scenario happens regularly at many workplaces. Is such miscommunication an intentional way of managing ? Not as a rule but still it happens. The sad part of the situation is that the boss has the last word, whether right or wrong, on such matters.

At the initial start of a new job practically everyone has respect for the boss. With the passage of time, however, the sheen of respect tends to be tarnished as the less than perfect traits of the boss become transparent. Quite a few supervisors make matters worse by their actions, such as confusing instructions or contradictory directives or broken personal promises. Needless to say such scenarios could have been easily resolved had the details been put in writing. But this takes time and effort. Besides, **should anything go wrong, the boss has staff to blame.** Here is where staff can help themselves by making known any specific concerns to the boss before undertaking a task.

Staff can tell fairly well what's on the mind of the boss once they become acquainted with the personal mannerism of the boss. Having such insight helps to cope and keep out of harm's way, but not always. On the other hand, the boss often picks the more capable to handle difficult jobs. Incidentally, the person commonly overlooked, for such tasks, is the worker who will do a lousy job. Needless to say the boss may jest about this fact but rarely will this seemingly hapless person be given tough assignment. In spite of this scenario staff occasionally welcome the chance to work at something new. In today's business scene, whether ready or not, that happens constantly as technology and the global market rapidly fluctuate, shift and evolve. The result is that staff has to do the usual assignments plus adjusting to newly created ways and means. A common consequence is a backlog. Staff may, in the spirit of co-operation, try to cope as best they can. But the overall trend, whether intended or not, is for business to do more with less. Eventually the work environment may become so tense there is stress. Alas stress, given sufficient time, will cause personal ill-health. Getting angry over being overworked is not going to help. Furthermore, any attempt to clear the backlog, through extra hours and effort, might increase the work assigned. It's important, therefore, to decide, beforehand, what you intend to do with the extra work assigned. This includes considering any potential gain, immediate and long term, versus the impact on personal health. The choice is yours as to the gains and drawbacks, likewise the advantages and disadvantages. Whatever you decide on ought to be communicated to the boss in a calm and honest way. Don't let the boss have the pretence of not knowing about the stressful situation.

## FROM A POSITION OF POWER

*whose say is final*
*divide and conquer*
*knowing the character of the boss*

A supervisor tries to ensure that staff do the many incoming tasks in a timely fashion. Naturally, these tasks are much more than any one person can possible do in the time expected. That's why there is staff. How the work is doled out, of course, varies from one supervisor to the next. Each supervisor tends to do so in a manner which reflects a personal evaluation about the capability of each member on staff. Some are conscientious about an equitable sharing of work. Some are not. To compound the situation there could be a member of staff who firmly believes, perhaps stemming from personal knowledge and past experience, that a specific task ought to be theirs. This may be so but it is the supervisor who has the last word about who gets what. Alas, this is also true for any request made by staff on personal matters. Fortunately, a reasonable request is usually granted. But the fact remains that the boss has the last word.

Supervising staff entails dealing with individuals with talents, working habits and insights commonly unique to each. The challenge is to divide the many incoming tasks equitably amid such a motley crew. In some cases it can be difficult and tough. To make matters worse the people on staff are usually very observant about who gets what In addition, they notice the slightest favouritism even when it is unintentional. Trying to rationalize a reasonable distribution of work can be, for a supervisor, a losing cause especially among staff of equal rank and pay. To deflect from such discretionary calls a supervisor might focus the attention of staff upon the shortcomings of a few. This tact is to make staff take comfort in thinking *thank goodness it's not me*. In other words, what the boss wants staff mostly to contemplate about is just their own individual self-interest and welfare. It is a case of the boss applying a Machiavellian concept of control - **divide and conquer**.

Anyone who is working understands that the balance of power tips in the favour of the boss. In spite of this a worker may become so upset about a seemingly unjust action by the boss that the urge is for, maybe demand, personal retribution. Here is where a worker ought to be cautious. For one, upper management will give the boss, at least initially, the benefit of the doubt. In many instances upper management will support the boss whether right or wrong. Here is where a worker, before complaining, needs to know intimately the ways and thinking of both the boss and the upper organization. It is much like knowing, in all respect, the style of the player being faced on a tennis court. Only then would you know how to stay away from the other player's strengths as well as how to utilize the other player's weaknesses. In fact by knowing and understanding the characteristic traits of the boss as well as the organization there is enhanced one's craft to communicate an effective message.

## BEING FAIR TO THE BOSS

*more power to the boss*
*fighting fire with fire*
*a joint effort*

Imagine, for a moment, your boss going through a day at work with no staff. How much would get done ? There will be very few managers who would be able to cope for the day. Most would do what they can - delaying whatever possible, attending to the most urgent matter, and so on. Should this continue for a week then output, naturally, will suffer. There even might be a personal panic attack. This imaginary scenario gives an idea of how helpful staff are. By doing assignments, in a timely fashion, staff are indirectly telling the boss that they can handle whatever tasks assigned. But this, in turn, may make a boss become imbued with an exaggerated sense of personal power. There might be even an inflated idea that staff can do more. In turn the boss may deem staff capable of doing tasks out of the ordinary. And so, without any qualms such tasks are assigned. Whenever this happens staff ought to point out the unusual nature of the demand, if necessary in writing, and query about extra compensation. Should such demands escalate, without appropriate compensation, then one must consider taking personal action, including moving on and out, rather than allow such an imposition without appropriate personal gain.

No matter how copacetic a work environment might be there will be an occasional frustrating moment. The natural inclination is to vent the ensuing rage on the perceived perpetrator. Often, however, the cause of one's wrath is the boss. So why should such an intrusive behaviour, boss or not, be tolerated ? Because by letting loose the rage within you will likely also let go of any self-control. Given the circumstance your subsequent action very likely will be filled with malice. Except for a passing moment of relief, however, there may be nothing more to gain. But there may be a lot to lose. Later the boss may become vindictive. Perhaps you could lose a potential promotion, even your livelihood. But to forego any form of retaliation is emotionally difficult. To do so involves waiting in hope for redress or, at least, an apology. Instead be prepared for an unfavourable outcome. As to the incident, one may think little of the boss behaviour but the moment cannot be forgotten. Let such an incident be a warning to keep one's distance from the boss whenever the boss seems incline to a tirade or a vindictive mood.

It is up to a supervisor to co-ordinate the various activities of staff - assigning work, monitoring works-in-progress, deciding what to do next and so on. In summary, the supervisor is responsible for the overall performance of staff. Often, in this respect, likely for expediency, a supervisor makes a cursory glance to a pending task before assigning it. Any critical issues likely will not become evident until staff takes a closer look at the job. Any critical issues then noted ought to be discussed with the boss. Here is where a worker might suggest what to do. Any decision then taken ought to be joint one. A word of caution: any oversight subsequently noticed could be a blame game. To avoid such potential scenario there ought to be consideration to put into writing any joint decision before proceeding.

## IT'S UP TO THE MANAGER

*morale*
*dialogue and morale*

It is, ultimately, the duty of a supervisor to tell staff what to do and, if need be, how to do a task. This is likely what happens when someone just start working but, after a while, the protocol gradually fades to a brief verbal exchange. Thus a task thereafter is assigned hardly with set instructions, much less guidance. Rarely will the supervisor become involved unless there is difficulty. How this is then addressed could be an issue. Staff may prefer the boss to decide what to do but the supervisor might desire staff to show initiative by resolving the issue alone. Should staff decline to take action then the boss must become involved. As a matter of fact, it is the duty of a supervisor to lead whenever need be. Leadership is inherent with every position of management. It is through leadership, or a lack of it, that the stewardship of the boss is viewed. In this respect, the stewardship, in the opinion of staff, may vary between total confidence to utter sarcasm. Where, on this spectrum, this opinion is located depends, of course, on a supervisor. As to ascertaining the actual point on the spectrum, that can be gleaned from the casual conversations of staff. Just eavesdrop on such informal talks and you can tell. What counts with leadership is how it affects the morale of staff. With trust and confidence staff have a high morale while sarcasm and ridicule commonly create poor morale.

Once a task is assigned it is the duty of the boss to monitor the works in progress. In turn the duty of staff is to tell the boss once troublesome issues are encountered. But, at times, staff ignores this aspect until it becomes a crisis. To avoid such impasse a supervisor ought to have one-on-one dialogue with staff, in a casual manner, frequently. Who knows, a worker may be experiencing personal problems thus affecting performance. Through dialogue a supervisor could detect such troublesome scenario. Here, in general, is where the tone and demeanour of a supervisor count. By being encouraging a supervisor could spark an open interactive relationship, while by being unduly fault-finding staff might become reluctant to talk about any difficulty whether on the job or with personal affairs. Any such reluctance could lead to a misunderstanding between supervisor and worker. For instance, staff may misread in a malicious way a well-intended directive of the boss. It is important, therefore, for a supervisor to take the initiative and maintain an open line of communication with each member of staff.

# DIFFERING POINT OF VIEW

*self interest*
*camaraderie*
*third party involvement*

No matter what action a person takes it is done with a set purpose in mind. Not always, of course, will this purpose be logical or well thought out. It could be an emotional response or a reflex reaction to circumstance or even for an aberrant personal motive. For instance, people react, without thinking, to help those in distress. Rarely do we think about the set purpose of another's action unless we are somehow impacted. Where the motive is readily apparent, and seems acceptable, then likely the situation ends there. In the work environment, however, the intent behind a corporate business action is commonly scrutinized. Gone are the days when most workers willingly do extra tasks without considering what is there to gain. Now self-interest seems to be the norm. So should you be doing, on a regular basis, specialized corporate tasks without being compensated properly then you ought to say so to the boss. Otherwise, without complaining, the situation likely will continue. Hopefully, it is resolved to your satisfaction. This could result in uncalled-for personal stress.

The difficulty of a task seems to depend often on who gives out the task and who has to do it. For instance, a supervisor may consider it a simple chore. But to the person who gets the task there could be trepidation. Here is where a supervisor could alleviate partially the tension. Here is where a boss, at the time of assigning the task, can reassure staff, on a personal note, that any unusual problem encountered should be discussed. But, alas, some supervisors seem to expect staff to resolve such issues on their own. After all, in some supervisors' perspective, that's what staff are being paid to do. Such managers can be found among those who attend business seminars and lectures addressing how to increase productivity. Well, without fostering morale amid staff the idea of greater productivity may be just wishful thinking.

Quite often a boss is depicted to be intolerant - an inconsiderate overseer, a slave driver, a despicable devil, an evil to be tolerated, maybe even the enemy. But this might not reflect the true personality of the boss. Who knows, the boss may personally believe that staff and supervisor ought to work together as a team. As for seemingly being intolerant, this could stem from the boss adhering religiously to corporate policy without a thought about how the action impacts staff. In other words, the boss is just doing her/his job the company seemingly demands. After all, a supervisor has to answer to a boss as well. Each unit of staff and supervisor in the organizational pyramid is just one nucleus of many. In that respect each time the boss meets with staff there is involved always a silent third party, namely, the organization. At such meetings it is the interest of the organization that matters. As a result the boss, now and then, may make greater demands. But the boss might be just following orders from above. Similarly, the boss might seem to make demands beyond acceptable ethical and social codes. The question is whether such actions stem from a personal style or a corporate directive. To secure an explanation it is up to the worker to so question each apparent impropriety the boss takes. Keep in mind that an organization wants to project a public image of being reasonable, ethical and, more importantly, values staff. Without such probing queries unreasonable demands likely will continue.

## TAKING A PERSONAL INTEREST

> *getting along*
> *getting the tasks done*
> *voicing one's concerns*

Getting along with others seems to be, for some, easy and natural. Such a disposition allows them to be at ease, as well as friendly, with both co-workers and management. In contrast are those with reticent behaviour who display a bit of discomfort dealing with others. No matter what kind of disposition a person has, however, each individual ought to try and foster a positive relationship with the boss. Here is a relationship which, over time, will become so close that one could likely finish a sentence the other started. So there is hardly anything one can mentally hide from the other. Hence there should be no hesitation to express, in a calm and reasonable fashion, any concern or an opinion that differs. At the same time one ought to accept, once you have made your opinion known, whatever the boss decides. Hopefully, the boss will show understanding and consideration to any concern so raised. No matter what is decided you ought to co-operate should the request be reasonable. If you are still uneasy then consider putting your opinion in writing before doing what's asked.

Within an organization there are two groups of people: those who decide what to do and those who do the work; in other words supervisors and staff. So the role of a boss is to get staff to do a certain set of tasks. In turn staff are expected to do them in a reasonable time. But sometimes this does not happen. Such incidents often create friction between supervisors and staff for what may seem reasonable to a supervisor may not be so to staff. There could arise, for example, problems out of the ordinary. For a dedicated few workers the tendency is to put in whatever extra effort needed without complaining. But quite often this action let the boss believe the same will be done in the future. Here is where an individual has to inform the boss about any setback due to the difficulty encountered and the extra effort made. This, perhaps, could be furthest from the supervisor's mind. Through an open-end dialogue at the start such misunderstanding can be avoided.

One working relationship that a person should devote time and effort is the symbiotic alliance with the boss. Often times, however, this alliance evolves into one of hostility. What seems forgotten is the working relationship at the initial start of the alliance. At that time a person, being new, commonly tries her/his best. This translates into being attentive and focused. At this stage the boss did the talking and one paid attention. It was common not to offer any dissenting opinion except constructive ones. Minor inconveniences and hardships were tolerated. This, however, could have conveyed a misconstrued notion of continued co-operation to the boss. In essence a passive role may give the boss the impression that any added demand is not a problem. So the earlier you let the boss know about the increasing backlog of work then this ought to clarify why tasks will take longer to do.

## TACT

*a show of force*
*about a power play*
*the blame game*

Sometimes the joy of working at a comfortable pace may slowly give way to a stressful state once there is a backlog of work. A nagging reminder by the boss to work harder, under the circumstance, can make matters worse. The resulting havoc could cause a few to become paranoid. Any further prodding, by the boss, might increase the paranoia. One may feel an urge to scream vile remarks, to lash back, even with physical blows. But, if you ever do so, more than likely you will be the one, in the end, who gets hurt. It is a waste of effort to take out one's frustration on those in power as they possess the upper hand. So just think of the stressful situation as an incident that will eventually pass. As for any agitated behaviour, you may be surprised to find out that those in power often greet it with glee. Here is an opportunity for them to show who is really in control and who has the final say. The malicious use of power tends to give an adrenaline rush. Such misuse of power is, I am told, narcotic. Thus challenging management in any manner likely brings out the worst in them. Moreover those in power seem to firmly believe that they can do no wrong governing staff. So just bridle the feeling within to retaliate with force. Just let the emotionally charged moment pass. Wait for another day and an opportune moment to lash back.

One aspect of human nature that will never change is that we all make mistakes. Often this happens due to an error in judgement. Even the boss occasionally make such a mistake. But, if repeated often, it might be a sign of incompetence. Be careful about whom you deem to be the cause, because the mistake might be due to upper management. Furthermore people in power don't like to be shown up. Here is a true story of how far people in power will go. Nearly two thousand years ago there lived a genteel charismatic man who preached about love. It is said that he could also do miracles. Why, on one occasion he supposedly fed a throng of five thousand with just five loaves and two fishes. He was so admired by his followers that they wanted to make him their king. Now all this adulation did not please a clique of clerics in authority. So the clique plotted and schemed to end his influence and sway. They seized the opportunity when one of his disciples desired to betray the charismatic leader for thirty pieces of silver. Once in captivity he was flogged and mocked. Bothered by the cruelty meted out, the forlorn disciple admitted betraying an innocent man and even gave back the silver coins. But by then the clique had gained total control. Knowing the letter of the law they orchestrated a trial leading to cross-carrying humiliation and public crucifixion. This is a case of how far some people in power will go to show who is in charge and control. So be careful about showing up someone in power especially at the workplace.

A commonly expressed sentiment of staff is that the boss divides up the workload unfairly. And very likely this is so. Each individual is only capable of doing so much and that ability varies from one person to the next. Knowing the capability of each staff member, a supervisor more than likely doles out work accordingly. If this seems unfair then it probably stems from what was done the first day on the job. Then you eagerly wanted to show what you could do. That's when the boss found out what you are capable of doing. Now, why do you think the boss is being unreasonable about what to expect from you ? There is nothing wrong in trying to do your best at the start. That is natural. We all do it, well, nearly all of us. What ought to be done at the start is to size up the boss. For that you will have to trust your instinct. This is also the best time to ask the boss about what's expected of you. It is at this point in time that the boss will be most co-operative and helpful. It is also at this point in time that you will be establishing how much the boss can depend on you. So any thoughts now about the boss being unfair seem to be more a complaint rather than a legitimate grouse. Too bad you weren't aware of this at the start of the job. Now it is a matter of putting into place gradually and slowly a comfortable pace doing work.

## CONSIDERATION

*having consideration*
*about trust*
*an alliance*

Being self-centred in whatever is pursued comes instinctively. Having consideration for others, however, is another story. Consideration for others takes a conscious effort. In this respect staff expect the boss to show a degree of consideration and concern. But, alas, as many can testify, there are supervisors who make no such allowance. But should the boss show no consideration then more than likely no one else in management will. Besides, who else but the boss is there better to validate, to upper management, any concerns staff may have ? Unfortunately, quite a few supervisors believe that their job is to do the will of the organization no matter what the impact is on staff. Moreover it is the duty of supervisors not only to communicate what upper management has to tell staff but also what staff wants to convey to upper management. If the boss decline to relay the concerns of staff to upper management then this merely underscores the poor leadership of a boss.

An organization depends on those on staff to do the corporate work so as to function effectively. In that respect every individual and every group within the organization has a defined role to play. Thus, within each working group, the role of staff is to aid and abet a supervisor in doing the work assigned to the unit. In turn the supervisor is responsible to oversee properly the work done. In other words, supervisor and staff are involved in a joint effort. That is the quest. Of course, in any constructive joint effort there ought to be a spirit of co-operation. But often self-serving personal agenda and egos get in the way. The result is a haphazard relationship of give and take. Still, the spirit of co-operation can prevail if consideration and trust be shown. Naturally, the first person who ought to show such qualities is the supervisor. Alas in many cases this is not likely to happen.

For the usual day-to-day tasks a supervisor has it relatively easy – since staff know what to do. The task of a supervisor is to co-ordinate these activities. As for those running the organization, namely senior management, their priority is to actively adjust these activities to the ebbs and flows of the market demands. This translates into shifting workloads as detailed in periodical directives from upper management. How a supervisor relays these to staff is a challenge because every one of us has a natural resistance to change. So a supervisor may not be comfortable telling staff about the new order of business. Ideally, however, both staff and supervisor could study each new protocol and comment constructively on how this affects them as well as to suggest modifications for the better. Naturally, it is the duty of the supervisor to relay these onto upper management. Whatever action upper management decide thereafter is not as crucial as the fact that there was a joint meeting of the minds between staff and supervisor. Alas, this happens all too seldom, likely because such joint action is furthest from the thinking of many supervisors.

## SPEAKING WITH STAFF

*the tone tells it all*
*transferring an idea to staff*
*a matter of trust*

Managing staff effectively takes more than mere goverance. There is also an element of psychology. This comes into play whenever the boss communicates with staff. What it takes is a skilful use, and choice, of words. Just give a thought about how a parent speaks to a child. Notice how the child reacts positively to a tone warm and supportive. But the reaction often is the opposite for a tone harsh and abrupt. In general, the tone of voice reflects a speaker's attitude towards the listener. In slavery days of the past it probably was discerned in the master's voice to a servant. Nowadays it is likewise discerned in the tone of a supervisor's voice. Thus the tone a supervisor employs with fellow managers could be quite different from the one used speaking to staff. Quite a few supervisors seem to convey a tone somewhat doubting or demanding or uncaring. Probably they want to project, intended or not, an attitude that there is no need to be polite to staff. Yet often these same supervisors desire, even demand, respect from staff. Sensing such a desire staff often respond with a show of respect. Alas, it may be merely superficial. What such supervisors need to realize is that respect cannot be demanded, rather it has to be earned.

With the passage of time, and job exposure, a newly appointed supervisor learns the protocols and process of the working unit being managed. Thereafter it is likely a matter of common sense and discretion. In the course of time there will be initiated, now and then, change probably brought about by new technology, a corporate directive or perhaps even a supervisor's discretionary call. Here is where a boss has an opportunity to show leadership. Before such an initiative is implemented the boss ought to call a meeting to discuss the proposed change with staff. This allows staff to ask any probing questions. Often times staff will give meaningful feedback as to potential glitches, even suggest possible solutions. Such a meeting, however, may seem a waste of time by supervisory personnel. Well, such a meeting, from the viewpoint of staff, would be informative and constructive. The interaction also helps camaraderie, not to mention being a potential showcase of leadership by the boss.

There is a degree of trust inherent in any working relationship. In times of old, even today, some people do business on a mere verbal agreement - no written contract with paragraphs of fine print. The spoken word given was good enough, their word was their bond. In the business world of today, however, written agreements are the norm. After all, it is strictly business. But the same cannot be said of the human dynamics between boss and staff, it is more like a partnership. This is why the word of a boss ought to reflect a degree of trustworthiness. In fact, it is common for staff, at the start, to trust the word of the boss. Thereafter it is up to the boss to take this trust and build on it. An effective way to do so is to communicate openly with staff. In other words it takes the actions of a boss to lose the trust of staff.

## PERSONAL AGENDA

*what counts most*
*in transition*
*handling change*

In the working arena it is natural to seek out a lucrative job. For most this entails well paid wages and benefits. Fortunately these issues are commonly negotiated by unions. If not, then the skill and experience a person presently has will be paid according to the competitive demand of the business world. Even among working peers some will endeavour to gain a better work cubicle, perhaps extra training and even vocational seminars. As for many supervisors, it is likely corporate recognition, perhaps a promotion. With such differing motives people work together as a productive unit. What they often overlook is the interest of a third party, namely, the organization. It must be said that each working unit of staff and supervisor functions strictly in the interest of the organization no matter how profitable a group may be. Ultimately only the interest of the organization is paramount.

A common trait of human nature is to take a familiar set of chores for granted. This includes one's work routines. But, like most human endeavours, that commonly change with the times. And so, one day, those in charge will simply make changes. Of course, there is a transition period between the old ways and the new. Nowadays a common change is a new computer program or upgrading the computers in use. Often during the transition stage there will be a glitch or oversight. Sometimes the new way excludes intricate steps used in the past. In addition, related training sometimes is poorly scheduled. Needless to say other glitches can, and do, happen. As far as upper management may be concerned, however, it was adequately planned with any glitch a minor issue and so easily resolved. But staff may beg to differ. Already changing to the new way likely created tension and stress. In addition, each mishap during transition causes added frustration and work disruption. Here is where the boss must help staff out. Here is where staff ought to be reassured not to be flustered. More importantly, the boss ought to keep upper management inform as to any unanticipated delay to the processing of work. Also the boss ought to say when the unit will be back to normal operation. This may seem a daunting task but no one else but the boss is in a position to do so.

Survival in the working world involves more than a job. A person ought to realize that each day in the global market new jobs are created while some existing ones are discarded. Similarly new working units are established and some are dissolved. Furthermore, as the years pass, new organizations come into being while some are dissolved. Thus there is no guarantee that the present job one has will be there as long as desired. And so personal attention needs to be paid as to the economic market for the organization where one works. As long as there is a sector demand then the organization likely will be in business. Likewise one has to pay attention to the economic market for the type of work one is doing. As long as there is a market demand for such personnel then there is a potential position elsewhere. A common source for such information is the newspapers especially the business sections as well as specialized journals. Another source is what those at work, especially in management, have to say about business in general. But many tend to dismiss negative news. Maybe they hope only for the better. But hope alone cannot sustain the continuation of the job at hand. Personally one ought to be ready for a "worst case" scenario. One ought to develop a tentative plan of action should the inevitable happen. To be thus prepared may likely lessen the trauma of any such disheartening news.

## 'PLAN B'

*if all else fails*

The art of communication is what we employ to let others know what we have in mind. Many times, after we express our mind, we expect the other party to respect our position and act accordingly. However there will be instances whereby the other party hears what you say but wants to do otherwise. Such is the situation whenever the reply includes **Yes.....but.....** It is a remark that seems to convey, initially, the listener's agreement - *Yes, I agree with you.* Yet there is a somewhat contrariant comment - *But that is not of importance.* It sounds as if you have the listener's sympathy but your opinion may not matter. So say no more. To voice any further comment likely brings more words of rebuttal that might make you become hot under the collar. It is therefore better to keep quiet particularly if the other party is your boss. Keep your lips zipped, stay calm and listen like a recording machine. Should the speaker be your boss then you are a captive audience. Listening to such words of provocation is part of the job. Who knows, maybe the boss wants to upset you deliberately. More reason why you should reply with just a glazed smile. So save your energy rather than waste it uselessly.

There likely will be a time when you set out to do just what the boss wants, as exact and precise as possible. But the result might turn out not to be what the boss wants. Guess who shoulders the blame. Guess who is berated about not asking questions at the appropriate moment. It gets worse should this happen over and over. Here is what you should consider doing, step by step, next time.

PLAN A

1. Repeat in your own words, to the boss, what you think the job involves as well as the step-by-step tasks to be done. As an added precaution, if time permits, do so in writing.

2. Should there be more than one way to do the job then write down a list of these alternatives with what you think is the most appropriate at the top and the worst at the bottom. Add a note that you will start the job once you are told to do so.

3. Should the boss not reply within a reasonable time then leave a note that the suggestion at the top will be done unless told otherwise. Include a date and, if possible, the time when the job will be started.

4. Should the boss ignore all the above then just leave a note detailing what you are about to do and when it likely will be done.

But using Plan A is no guarantee that the boss will be pleased. In fact using this plan could cause untold trouble. Some people are never satisfied. If that happens then you may need to go to 'Plan B'. This is what cowboys of the wild west have in the back of their minds whenever they relax at saloons and bars. At these 'watering' holes play can get a bit rough as the evening wears on. Usually there will be drinking bouts and boastful bragging leading to tempers flaring. The outcome could be a shoot out duel next day at high noon. This is when a cowboy may consider using 'Plan B'. 'Plan B' is to simply get out of town. The modern day version of 'Plan B' is to start looking for another job. It is a plan of action that could allow one to retain personal sanity. It is pursued by holding on to the present job but to start actively searching for another place to work. By the way, you ought to keep such a search to yourself and tell no one. In the meantime ***Believe only half of what you see and little of what you hear***. Happy hunting.

## Supplement C - The Workplace

*knowing the routine*
*relating to others*
*reasonable resolution*
*being fair and equitable*

Working is a chore many consider to be a daily grind stretching several days a week. The difficulty, after a while, seems to be a lack of satisfaction with the job. Occasionally there is wishful thinking about doing something else but that's easier said than done. For there seems to be too many people chasing a better job. This includes those with many years of experience. As for the job of the moment, there was likely, at the beginning, novelty and interest with a positive attitude - alert, willingness to learn and eager to please. There was effort made to fit in and know the people at work. Then the novelty, and interest, somehow waned. This was compounded by the irritating habits of others in the workplace. So occasionally a work day seems longer than ever. It is no surprise, therefore, for the morale of many to perk up once they leave the confines of work. There kindles a desire to find a way to cope with the dismal effect of the work environment. That likely will take an understanding of the workings of an organization with the people and protocols therein.

With a new job there usually comes an arrear of new experiences - the work to do, the workplace protocols and people newly met to know. With the fresh faces at the workplace there commonly follows a varied arrear of friendships and alliances. One cultivates a working alliance often on an individual basis and perhaps a symbiotic degree of dependence. As for friendships in general, well that likely evolves once common interests become known. With like camaraderie workers tend to splinter into small social groups. As for the social protocols that tends to be valued in an organization, these can be ascertained by recognizing the traits in common shown by those in upper management. It does not matter what one may think but these traits most often are necessary to be successful in the organization.

Often times amid a group of workers there will be a few who pursue their job with enthusiasm and intensity. Somehow they seem to get more done. This phenomenon was confirmed in a time-and-motion study of blue-collar workers by F. W. Taylor several decades ago. The same can likely be said of any group of workers today. The hope of fellow workers is that these high performers slow their productive bent down to a reasonable norm. At the same time, however, management probably hope that others perform to a similar high output. Disenchantment likely follows. If only both sides accept the fact that such a high rate of productivity is a personal prerogative. The issue, likely for all parties, is what incentive should be given for such cases. Once agreed upon by all then there should be no further problem. Hopefully, the supervisor could coordinate such a discussion and understanding. In reality, however, no such action will likely be pursued. Instead each party will likely choose a course of action with self serving interest.

This is the conundrum encountered should one perceive a plausible and reasonable solution to an issue at work but which will not satisfy all parties involved. In such a situation you have no choice but to safeguard your own interest while awaiting management to resolve the matter.

In a small organization the people on staff get to know each other very well. In the process they learn the ways and habits of everyone to such an extent that each can tell the intention underlying personal actions. But as an organization grows such personal insight likely lessen; the larger the organization the more distant any personal contact. So much so that management often is discerned, especially by the lower echelon, as an impersonal icon with inanimate feeling. In reality, of course, the powers that be, in a sizeable organization, are far from robotic and inhumane. But the primary aim of their actions is the interest, and the survival, of the organization. Thus the goals of management can differ, and do, in many ways, from the personal goals of people working for the organization. An understanding of the structural fabric and hierarchical role of management might lessen any animosity an individual may have about adverse corporate decisions. Needless to say, there ought to be, but not always shown, a humane touch in putting decisions, adverse to staff, into action. That often is a personal prerogative of a supervisor.

## GROWING PHASES OF AN ORGANIZATION

Organizations come in different sizes and vary from a one person operation to a work force of thousands. To comprehend the different management mode of operation an attempt will be made to describe the growing phases going from a one person operation to a multi-force corporate body. Of course, an organization can be established, at the start, for any size privately or by public governance.

*a one man show*
*getting a bit of help*
*layering the work*
*huge and cumbersome*

Many who are working for others often dream that, one day, they hope to have a business of their own. Quite a few then do so alone - a one man, or woman, operation. By their lonesome self they do sales, services, logistics and whatever necessary to get the work done; much like someone walking alone. Such an individual decides what to do, where to go, when to go, how to get there, and what the journey is all about. But managing alone will involve business activities brand new and are done likely by trial and error. It is a learning process. Still, the challenge of being on one's own is a adventure many can't resist trying. For those who succeed there is ample reward and a degree of satisfaction. For those who fail they gain experience which make them realize that running an organization is not easy and not for everyone.

Quite often a one man, or woman, operation, with sustained success, has so much work that help is hired and, with time, this increases to a handful of people. What management has done is much like someone deciding to walk no longer and, instead, ride a bicycle. Now he, or she, can go to places faster and get more done with less effort. Members of staff are like the spokes and wheels on the bicycle. The role of staff is to help management move around quicker and better. In such a setting everyone on staff gets to know each other very well. In such a setting communication of ideas, opinions and intentions is not an issue for relationships tend to be informal and friendly with the workload often overlapping.

With an end product, or service, in increasing demand an organization might increase its workforce several hundred fold. Here the work now is spread over three layers of personnel: management, white collar staff and blue collar workers. Each person is assigned a set task, responsibility and authority. Collectively, they keep the organization running and humming. In this phase the management mode is to delegate rather than supervise personally. Now the interaction between management and workers tends to be minimal and formal except among close associates. To get an idea of the change in management style imagine the organization to be like someone putting aside a bicycle and, instead, drives a car. Management now focuses mainly on the steering to the destinations desired. The people working are now in two groups - supervisors and workers - and constitute the many moving parts under the bonnet of the car. Upper management now has hardly any time or energy to interact with staff. Now, for a worker, contact with management, for the better or the worse, is mainly through supervisors. Alas, upper management tends to overlook any bias in supervision until the situation spirals into a crisis. Part of the problem seems to be upper management promoting someone not capable. In other words, a mistake has been made and upper management is in denial. Often workers try to adjust to signs of incompetence such as poor judgement or indecisiveness. But only upper management, in the end, can remedy the situation.

As demand grows the workforce within an organization then might increase until it numbers in the thousands. Such a size will necessitate not only layers of staff but also separate divisions of authority for set activities such as production, sales and human resources. Naturally, the decision-making process will involve input of all divisions on matters of common interest. The usual process is to create a committee with representatives from each division. The norm for the committee is to deliberate and recommend a course of action to senior management for approval. Subsequent implementation has to be synchronized with all divisions and working units. Thus the organization now has to do large-scale systematic coordinated effort such as training and upgrades. The management mode for the organization is now is like someone who steps out of a car into the cockpit of a jumbo jet. Senior management is the team in the cockpit with a view of the commercial horizon. Now the perspective of these senior managers is to study the national and global market. It is for them to guide the organization through the shifting and undulating business landscape. As for the workforce, the many units and layers of management, staff and workers, they are like the plane's many supportive parts; such as turbo engines, fuel and ground support systems. These supportive groups keep the organization flying, the turbo engines spinning and, hopefully, whizzing along. They help to meet the looming challenges of the business world. An individual working within such an organization is merely a speck on the wings. But there may come that rare occasion when that speck shines like a diamond. Senior management might notice this sparkle and more than likely then reward the glitter of initiative shown.

## RUNNING AN ORGANIZATION

*a team effort*
*planning change*
*a co-operative effort*

Every organization has a purpose; whether that be to make widgets or to put a smile on the lips of contented cows. But it takes more than a purpose for an organization to function and to get the job done. It takes a primary driving force within the organization, a force that somehow keeps reinventing itself from one corporate objective to the next. Otherwise the organization, no matter how active and vibrant, eventually disintegrates and chaos follows. It is a force that knows how to employ power and people.

This force sustains the corporate vision about where to go and how to get there. This force decides whether the organization walks, rides or drives, perhaps even to go airborne. Often the driving force is a powerful individual atop of the organization. Usually the power is shared with a corporate team, such as a partnership or a Board of Directors. This energetic individual outlines the overall direction the organization takes. But getting the tasks done depends on the people below doing the necessary work. It is a symbiotic relationship. To illustrate this aspect let's consider a change to a present protocol within an organization. Suppose it is decided to put a new procedure in place. To do so there is prepared a plan of implementation. There is then staged and scheduled the necessary training and physical changes. Then the new strategy is employed. But for all these activities to be effective all units affected are consulted during the planning process. This consultation illustrates the symbiotic alliance.

There are constant changes happening in society. In like fashion organizations will change with the times. How the change is carried out commonly depends on the size of the organization. In a small organization management tends to tinker with these protocols until a suitable fit is reached. In a large organization, however, this is not easily done. There has to be a plan of action to ensure that the transition is coordinated so that any disruption to the usual functions of the organization is kept to a minimum. But often the coordination is shortchanged, perhaps by resources, maybe by lead time. A common oversight, in the process, is proper training of staff beforehand. Another shortfall is a lack of input, during the planning stage, from affected staff in the lower echelon. Likewise overlooked, surprisingly, is a bulletin to staff on why the change and what will be gained by the change. As a matter of fact poor communication on corporate matters tends to create low morale. In general the state of morale is usually reflected in what staff has to say about the organization.

To carry out organizational changes successfully there has to be a follow-through on all the details. In the planning stage management try to anticipate what likely will happen and, hopefully, the solutions; the more complex a project is, the more planning helps. At the beginning of executing the plan there is hardly any problem getting, for instance, from **C** to **D** of the plan. But further along the way, for instance from **P** to **Q,** the outcome might not be as anticipated. The challenge is for management to come up with an improvised solution to complete the process adequately. Often times, at this stage of the plan, staff is involved. In that regard a suggested course of action is to hold a brainstorm session with those affected. Drawing on their past experience they will likely discern a viable and practical solution. In reality, however, the implementation team often does what they believe is proper no matter how ill fitting it may be. In many cases, after the new system is in place, staff overrides that part of the new protocol with a better one. Naturally, this tends to create skepticism towards anything new by management. Management ought to consider carefully the input of staff during the planning stage. In other words, staff can be of valuable assistance in improving the running an organization if only management would pay attention and listen.

## MANAGERIAL DISCRETION

*influencing morale*
*ways of governance*
*a joint venture*

Every person, within an organization, has an identifiable job to do. Each has certain responsibilities and tasks; it might be to deliver widgets, or talk to clients, or to manage a work unit. By so doing each contributes to the functioning of the organization no matter where located on the corporate totem pole. With time, each can tell how best to get the related tasks done; what gets immediate attention, which can be done later. Unless the boss says otherwise. In that respect the boss is part of the equation in the running of the organization. In that regard the boss represents corporate power. As such it is the boss who can be, in the eyes of staff, a morale booster or a detractor. By being reasonable and understanding staff likely will be cooperative. But by being overbearing there commonly will be created animosity. The result is to cause staff to think less of the organization. As for those in control of the organization, they prefer a positive attitude rather than a dismal outlook. In this respect it is chiefly up to the boss to determine which point of view prevails. Such is the power and influence of a boss over the workers.

In the eyes of the workers the boss is discerned not as someone who also works for the same organization, but as management personified. Often times, in that role, the boss has to make a decision involving both the interest of the organization as well as that of staff. Often times a decision cannot benefit both. Rather one party tends to gain at the expense of the other. This is the plight the boss faces. Moreover whatever is decided has a ripple effect upon morale. In general the organization tends to focus on productivity while staff tends to desire doing less while demanding more. Sometimes the demand might be valid such as training or vocational seminar or bonus. Naturally, productivity will be the deciding factor. So the tendency is for a supervisor to assign as much as reasonable possible to those productive. As for the training, seminar or bonus, well a boss tends to reward those whom the boss considers cooperative and likely supportive. Often times workers wonder why upper management allows this bias behaviour to happen. This is likely because upper management is not aware of it. Should the situation be brought to attention of upper management then the supervisor likely will give a somewhat plausible explanation. Upper management tends to accept this explanation at face value. As for the person complaining, well she/he then is likely tagged a trouble maker. In the interim the boss continues with the same bias behaviour.

At times the boss is discerned to be someone who prevents a worker reaching full personal potential. But there was a time, at the start, when the boss was seen in a positive way. In those days the boss helped one to get started and become familiar with the job. Likewise, the boss was trusted in what was said and one did, whenever possible, whatever the boss asked. With time and experience there was gained self confidence. Now routine tasks are done as a second nature. Now and then better ways of doing the tasks might be discerned and implemented. But the boss may prefer that the established protocol be followed. Naturally, this reaction could cause resentment of the boss. With similar incidents happening in the future a worker likely will find faults in the behaviour of the boss. Now the boss is seen as an adversary rather than an ally. Pity. Imagine, for a moment, the possibility of boss and worker pooling resources, exchanging ideas freely and implementing ways to improve the process. Alas, such a thought may cause unintended consequences. Such joint actions would be, to some supervisors, a sharing of personal power. No way will these supervisors allow that to happen.

## MIDDLE MANAGERS

> *making decisions*
> *theory x*
> *theory y*
> *the organization personified*

Managing is a task which entails making a decision, now and then, with not enough information much less time. This can be stressful since whatever is decided likely includes a degree of uncertainty. But making decisions is part of the job. Managers, therefore, gladly welcome any momentary lull just by staff following the usual routine and putting out the customary predictable results. Such a break may bring a reflective moment. It is a moment, perhaps, to thoughtfully consider new ideas, to ponder on the novelty and concept of doing something else. Most times, however, the mind tends to wander elsewhere. Still, such reflective breaks give some relief to the job. But what many managers do not like is staff lapsing into such reflective reverie. Heaven forbids, but a few managers seem to prefer staff to be mindless creatures who robotically perform the tasks. As a matter of fact managers have imaginative notions about the various attitudes, good and bad, of staff.

There are some managers who believe that most workers, left on their own, do not have the interest of the organization at heart. They believe workers lack initiative, drive and a sense of responsibility. Workers are interested only in what they can squeeze out of the organization. In addition, workers are against any changes in the work routine that could get more done. As a result, they need to be treated, at times, like children - closely supervised and scrutinized. This well known classical management concept is commonly refer to as **theory x**.

There are some managers who believe that workers are conscientious, productive and cooperative should they be given proper tools: training, a comfortable work environment and fair wages. With such incentives workers will be motivated, attentive and responsible in their day to day work. The role of the manager is to be supportive and to get the tools and resources needed for staff to get the job done. This common management concept is known as **theory y**.

The many perspectives to managing, expressed and written, span from that of **don't trust at all** to that of **trusting completely**. Managers tend to have a point of view somewhat in between. Sometimes they lean one way and sometimes the other. To each worker, naturally, the viewpoint that matters most is that of the present boss. To nearly all workers their immediate boss IS management personified, the organization in totality. It is the boss who decides, for the organization, many matters for those on staff, such as what a person should do and any time off for personal affairs. Indeed, the boss represents, in such situations, the might and will of the organization. As a matter of fact the boss may be the only individual in a position of power with whom an individual ever deals. In that respect the boss can influence an individual to be positive and constructive about the job and the organization. On the other hand, any valid animosity an individual may have against the organization often stems from the bias actions, or lack of support, of the boss.

# NETWORKING

*camaraderie*
*friendly persuasion*
*the informal pathways*

Each working day people busily do their jobs with conscientious effort. The aim is to do a honest day work for a honest day pay. Although the main focus is upon the many tasks at hand there is also involved another aspect to work which many hardly give much thought. It is that work is also an arena of social activity where people talk and interact with each other. In the process they supplement, and compliment, the efforts of each other. In the process there is exchanged humour, ideas and opinions such as why individuals do the tasks the way it's done. In the process one learns the varied personalities of working associates. By being congenial in such interactions there is friendship and, more importantly, less misunderstanding. But many times such exchanges reflect differing points of view which could upset a few individuals. As a result these few may prefer to maintain a strict business like relationship with associates, with little congeniality, while advocating that only their personal opinion counts. At times it appears that this limited relationship is etched in stone. Such solitary perspective seems to leave hardly any room for what others think much less say. To make matters worse these solitary figures tend to stay away from any staff socials especially those outside of working hours. In today's work environment, however, camaraderie among workers often plays a key role to effective team effort. Such team effort is one segment to the network system in an organization.

A natural tendency of human behaviour is to avoid painful experiences. As a result we tend to keep away from people who make us uncomfortable. Thus we tend to have close friends with shared values and with whom we have a relaxing sense of comfort. This hardly is the case, however, with people who work together especially in a large organization. Here there usually are people from other cultures and diverse interests. Here one likely has to overcome any personal uncomfortable sentiment with such individuals and be, perhaps superficially, cordial and friendly. Here one likely explores interactive pathways to be congenial. It usually helps to reach out by exchanging information or by casual conversation. Thereafter it is a matter of being cooperative in the business agenda of the organization. Sometimes co-workers become social friends. Should no attempt be made to establish such a working relationship there, invariably, is a degree of suspicion and skepticism. Here is a case whereby it pays to be friendly. It is also a way of becoming part of the information network system known as the grape vine.

Many look on their job as merely a source for income. Rarely do they perceive the workplace as a social arena. Rarely do they realize that the interactive contacts with those at work are threads which weave a social network fabric commonly refer to as the informal organization. It is through such social contacts that one learns about the unwritten norms of an organization. Those who perceive that such contacts can be beneficial, personally, often explore interactive pathways beyond the setting of the workplace. So, with this in mind, they attend business parties, conferences, professional activities and even social clubs. What they hope to foster is a personal contact with influential people. This process is social networking. As a matter of fact the setting for the most powerful network group is within elite social clubs, such as the golf and country club. Here is where this group, the old boys network, gathers informally. The network probably grew out of informal business get-togethers at the turn of the twentieth century. The social values of those gathered commonly reflected the code of conduct then acceptable to society. It was a time when men went to work and women kept the home fire burning. It was a time when higher education was an arena crowded with the future leaders of society: white able bodied males. This is likely the source for the old boys nomenclature. As to joining the old boys network, well, membership was informal. Still is. No registration was necessary, just behaviour and attitude and perhaps schooling. Practically all organizations then, large and small, had people in positions of power culled from this clique, particularly business, institutions and government. The old boys club was, and still is, a loose social network. In a sense the sheen on this fabric could be, for a few, a cloak for personal comfort. Often the cloak is mistakenly deemed to be a blanket for trust. So much so that many members seem to have difficulty trusting people outside of the network group. But present circumstances are rapidly changing and, in the process, making the sheen of this fabric many hued. Trade and business has grown beyond the confines of a group of nations to an international worldly stage. To communicate and compete on this global landscape of today, people, especially managers, need to be highly flexible in dealing with the many different cultures, customs and social values. In such dealings one may, from time to time, need to set aside personal habits tried and true. Likewise people need to be flexible about changing the way things are done, at a moment's notice. The challenge now is to figure out whom to trust. For some it still is one's gut feeling. For other it is a matter of personal experience.

## ORGANIZATIONAL CULTURE

*a unique set of values*
*the influence of power*
*the unwritten behavioural rules*
*clasping the culture*

To some people all big business operate the same way. That is not so, in some respect they may seem to follow the same protocols but no two such organizations are managed in identical manner. True, organizations have certain elements in common - such as people with specialized skills, accountants, a network using computers and core business hours. For sure, all have ambitious people on staff as well as a few lackadaisical personnel. But each organization is somewhat unique such as the way they get things done with a protocol dictated by those managing the organization. To understand this concept let's take a moment to look at a familiar unit of society - the family. Common elements among most successful families are cars, televisions, expensive toys, and a home. But each element will differ from one family to the next. For instance, the home might be a luxurious apartment or a sprawling mansion; the cars likely vary in numbers, colour and types, and so on. The eventual combination of expensive toys and number of children varies from family to family. This is what makes each family unique. A uniqueness which is furthermore underscored by what they want out of life and what they value at heart. In other words, each family has a certain unique mind set as well. In much the same way each organization is unique particularly in the way they do business with clients and customers. Each seems to have a way that often crystallized the varying beliefs, opinions and interests of the people at the top. Each organization has a set of certain core values which is unique. So the type and degree of benevolence, as well as malevolence, varies from one organization to the next. To ignore this fact is a fallacy as well as being obstinate.

We commonly learn from others. A complementary aspect to this process is the influence others have on us. Such influence tends to sway us in how we act as well as in emotional outlook. In fact a few people seems capable of influencing a person just by their mere presence. As a matter of fact it is said that each person we meet influence us in some way, whether significantly or partially, positive or negative. A source of such influence, in the work arena, is people in positions of power. Maybe the hope is to be, one day, in a similar position of power. Here is a true story about such an influence. It is about someone who chaired the most powerful unit in an organization: the Board of Directors. Collectively, they decide how to run the organization. In any case the Chairman of the Board was an avid tennis devotee who played every single day. Once this became known within the organization most managers, junior and senior, took to the game. This love for the game continued as long as he was Chairman of the Board. But shortly after he retired tennis was no longer a corporate sport. What this demonstrates is that a manager can be a powerful influence on staff. Likewise note the fact that such influence ends whenever a manager goes.

It takes a certain kind of mentality to manage with confidence. This entails a logistic vision of what will likely unfold on the job and to plan appropriately. Of course, not everyone working is capable of doing so. Still, each worker can bring personal effort to the process and, collectively, get the job done. In an effective process the workforce commonly has a spirit of camaraderie and cooperation. Such kinship and equanimity is what a person cedes upon accepting a supervisory position from the lower ranks. The natural tendency is to then manage with equity balanced with personal values as to ethics, morality and fairness. Unless, of course, it is contrary to corporate policy and social codes. However such codes are rarely told directly to someone joining management. Such codes commonly pertain to ethical behaviour, attitude and norms arbitrarily expected within the organization. These are hardly ever put in writing. Worse yet, one may mistakenly deem them to be optional and thus ignores them. As a matter of fact, as long as a working unit is efficient and effective ignoring such expectations may not be an issue for a manager. hat might be a personal issue, however, is the absence of camaraderie and kinship once felt as a member of working staff. Believe it or not, such comrade kinship exists within managerial ranks. The difference is that there is one clique in management while there are likely many cliques amid staff and workers. As one can imagine, each clique consists of individuals with shared values and interests. There might even be common sentiments as to beliefs, opinions and biases. It is a matter of just finding, amid staff and workers, a clique to one's level of personal comfort. Among managerial ranks, however, a person has a choice of either joining this established clique or be somewhat socially isolated. As to the managerial clique, it originated very likely along with the organization. Furthermore, the social characteristics are somewhat set as to behavior, norms, ethics, shared values and perhaps biases. To discern these characteristics just view the personal actions of those in positions of power and influence, just listen to what they say. These characteristics commonly tantamounts to an ***organizational culture***. Often times it is this culture that changes the personality of someone promoted from staff into managerial ranks. The change might be for the better but it could be for the worse.

In our day to day living we recognize the various creeds, customs and rituals that are in society. Each of us has learn how to adjust to these various forms. As for work, most of us go through the motion, try our best and somehow cope. It is now time to perceive and accept that the workplace, especially in a large corporate body, is also an arena of social interactions. As such it is a society of sort. In fact, for each of us it is a significant society in our life. It is now time to admit that, whether we like it or not, there are certain creeds, customs and rituals adherent to the organization where we work. This translates into certain behaviour, norms, shared values, acceptable actions and beliefs, perhaps even opinions. These are the codes arbitrarily governing this society of work. All this is practically not in writing. With time we gain insights to this social system by observing and interacting with those in power, influence perhaps experience. With this knowledge you can then try to develop a personal plan to somehow adjust to the organizational culture at work. Keep in mind this world is far from ideal and that includes each and every organization. So organizations are rarely structured ideally and rarely run perfectly. So be prepared for limitations to your personal expectations. Trust that your organization culture is compatible with your expectations. Otherwise it is a matter of accepting the situation and coping. Either way you now ought to have an idea of why things are done a certain way at work. Now it is a matter of deciding what's best for your interest..

# Selected Bibliography

## STRESS

Markham, Ursula *Managing Stress*
Element, Inc. Rockport, MA 1995

Orman, Mort *THE 14 DAY STRESS CURE*
Breakthru Publishing Houston, TX 1991

Green, W.J. *Fatigue Free* Plenum Press New York, NY    1992

## DEADLY SINS

Sunday Times Publications Ltd. *The Seven Deadly*          *Sins*
BOOKS FOR LIBRARIES PRESS Freeport, New York 1962

Anthony Campolo *Seven Deadly Sins*
SP Publications, Inc. Wheaton, Illinois 60187 1989

Henry Fairlie *The Seven Deadly Sins Today*
Simon and Schuster New York, New York 10020 1978

## CONTROL

Andrew P. Morrison *The Culture of Shame*
Random House of Canada Limited, Toronto 1996

Vincent Mosco *the PAY-PER-SOCIETY*
Garamond Press 67A Portland Street Toronto, Canada 1989

## WORK

Peter M. Blau *Bureaucracy in Modern Society*
Random House New York 1968

Peter M. Blau and Richard Scott *Formal Organizations*
Chandler Publishing Company San Francisco 1962

Albert J. Bernstein and Sydney Craft Rozen *Sacred Bull* John Wiley & Sons, Inc. Toronto 1994

Usula Markham *How to Survive without a Job* Judy Piatkus (Publishers) Ltd. London W1P 1HF 1994

Keith Davis and John W. Newstrom *Human Behaviour at Work* McGraw-Hill Publishing Company Toronto 1989

Kenichi Ohmae *The Borderless World*
Harper Business 10 E. 53rd St. New York, NY 1990

Robert Howard *Brave New Workplace* Penguin Books Canada Limited 2801 John Street Markham, Ontario Canada L3R 1B4 1985

Ferdinand F. Fournies *Why Employees Don't do what they're supposed to do and what to do about it* Liberty Hall Press 1988

# Index

Made in the USA